LILLIAN TOO'S
168 Feng Shui Ways to a Calm and Happy Life

LILLIAN TOO'S
168 Feng Shui Ways to a
Calm and
Happy Life

CICO BOOKS
London

Published in Great Britain by Cico Books Ltd
32 Great Sutton Street
London EC1V 0NB

(+44) 20 7253 7960

For image credits, see page 160.

ISBN 1-904991-26-2

10 9 8 7 6 5 4 3 2

Design: Jerry Goldie
Project editor: Liz Dean
Illustrators: Stephen Dew, Kate Simunek,
Anthony Duke

Printed in China

Contents

Part Two
Creating a Powerfully Auspicious and Happy Home

Part Three
Safeguarding the Home

INTRODUCTION

The wonderful thing about feng shui is the positive benefit it creates for everyone. Feng shui is not just about becoming wealthy or achieving success – it is concerned with enriching lives, reducing aggravations, and bringing happiness into relationships. It is about feeling happy, prosperous, and contented.

When you know how to orientate your doors, organize the layout of rooms, arrange furniture, and be creative in the use of colors, shapes, and materials, and know about the placement of decorative items in your home, you will discover a new energy and zest for life. Life becomes more joyous, your relationships with loved ones reach deeper levels of understanding, and interactions with siblings and close friends, as well as those between the different generations living in the home, begin to improve out of sight. And if you also know how to keep your feng shui up-to-date from year to year, the benefits will be even more amazing. When your home enjoys good feng shui, it literally becomes infused with harmonious, joyous energy, and in such an atmosphere general health is much improved. And the benefits reach out beyond the walls of your home, infusing your wider social circle with the same positive energy. With the home happy and calm, blissful and restful, it becomes a real haven, a sanctuary – just as a home should be.

Why does feng shui work?

Once your spatial energy is positive and auspicious, filled with good vibes, any feelings you may have of stagnation and despair become a thing of the past – and what you feel often reflects the energy of your home. A tense and angry state of mind is often a sign that the energy around your home is not synchronized, and is disharmonious. A sad and unhappy disposition also suggests that the invisible and intangible chi of your home is disturbed or feeble, and in need of fresh "oomph."

Physical afflictions

Spatial feng shui is easy to take care of. The rule is to keep the chi moving – never let it stagnate or become unbalanced. Sound, activity, movement, and people all keep chi in motion, yet too much yang chi can also be quite unbalancing. So it is necessary to guard against overdoing any feng shui recommendations you decide to implement.

When space stays too still and is neglected for a period of time, vibrant chi stagnates. To wake it from its passive sleep-state, you need to move your furniture around. Just shifting your sofas a few feet out and cleaning their backs, and moving your coffee tables and cleaning under them before moving them back into place, will cause the chi energy to transform and become revitalized, even if temporarily (see Tip 29). Incorporating space-cleansing and feng shui purification rituals will make the process even more effective (see my book *168 Feng Shui Ways to Declutter Your Home*). However, the mere act of moving the furniture will shift the chi energy, making you feel much better.

Spatial feng shui requires you to stay alert to the physical afflictions that bring unfortunate luck, afflictions that can usually be found in almost every house. Different things cause physical afflictions, and you will find many examples in this book, together with suggested cures and remedies. The arrangement of home space is something many of us take too much for granted, focusing our attention purely on the aesthetic aspects of arrangement and décor. Thus, with insufficient consideration being given to feng shui design implications, correct feng shui inputs can improve the luck of almost every home, irrespective of the style of decoration.

What is important is to remain sensitive to physical structures, colors, shapes, pillars, beams, art pieces, and decorative items within the space. These often result in the type of feng shui problems that make life difficult and aggravating – such as causing anybody living in the house to grow annoyed or become frustrated far more quickly than usual.

At its worse, bad feng shui leads to anger, loss, and even violence. The severity of bad feng shui depends on whether the negative energy is merely weak, or is negative to the point of being "killing" and thus harmful. Even worse, it may be "dead," in which case it needs to be revived. These three types of negative chi bring misfortunes and unhappiness. Bad feng shui in the home means that all three types of negatives are present, causing you problems. The causes of such energy in your home must therefore be addressed and attended to, otherwise you will continue to suffer difficult and angry times.

The Element Cycles

In feng shui there are five elements: water, metal, earth, fire, and wood, and three element cycles – productive, exhaustive, and destructive. Each compass sector, astrological animal sign, and period of time has an associated element.

Time afflictions

The other aspect of feng shui that must be investigated has to do with time. While physical afflictions are the result of placement, design, blockages, and orientations, time afflictions are the result of the passing of time. There are, therefore, two dimensions to the influences of feng shui – space and time – and to ensure that you make the best of time chi, you need to update your feng shui in accordance with changing time periods, and also with the feng shui calendar from year to year.

The Chinese place great emphasis on the calendar. The main Chinese calendar is the lunar calendar, which is expressed as the "stems and branches" of time. Each cycle of calendar time is expressed in terms of the five elements – water, wood, fire, earth, or metal (the "heavenly stems") – as well as the 12 animals (the

"earthly branches"). Each big cycle that combines stems and branches lasts 60 years.

As we move from one year to the next, chi energy changes, transforming from yin to yang, from element to element, and from one animal sign to the next. Depending on whether the months and years are yin or yang, water, fire, metal, earth, or wood, and also depending on what animal sign it is, the chi energy of homes and of personalities also changes.

Thus, time exerts a very strong impact on your feng shui, on your luck, and also on your destiny. Good feng shui cannot and does not last forever. It has to be recharged with small but significant changes every year. Energy must be refreshed, reorganized, and re-energized. Spaces and places need rejuvenating. Chi must be kept moving.

Period 8 new chi

In addition to the lunar calendar, the Chinese also have the Hsia calendar, which is used for demarcating months and years with a view to practicing the more advanced compass formulas of feng shui. Specifically it is used in the practice of the flying star formula – a technical approach to feng shui that addresses directly the effect of time on the chi energy of homes.

We are currently in the 20-year period ruled by the number 8. We entered this new period of 8 on February 4, 2004. Hence, the year 2004 was a benchmark year for many people and for many countries. With the change of period comes a change of energy.

Prior to February 4, 2004, the world was influenced by the energy of metal, when the pursuit of wealth overshadowed most other aspirations. Plenty of money was made from metal energy, especially in the United States – think of Bill Gates and the rise of Microsoft, along with developments in computer technology. But period 7 ended in 2004, and in this year many countries experienced upheaval – the USA, China, Australia, Indonesia, India, Spain, Malaysia, Singapore, and the Philippines all experienced leadership changes or renewals. This was felt at the macro and micro level, in the corridors of national governments as well as in individual households and offices around the world.

With the period change, houses built in the previous period 7 experienced a weakening of their vitality. All buildings constructed before February 2004 should, ideally, be changed to period 8, or at least have their chi energy revitalized and replenished.

Changing to period 8

Changing to period 8 is sure to benefit all homes. If the transformation is made in accordance with the new period flying star charts (see Tip 38) the benefits will be even more dramatic. Contained within this book is all the information you need.

Updating your feng shui automatically rebalances the yin and yang attributes of any home, because implicit in the transformation will be a new door, new floor, and a new roof, which replenishes the trinity of chi (heaven, earth, and human-kind chi – see Tip 63). These are the requirements for changing the period of any house.

With the introduction of the new chi, conflicting energies are systematically reduced. Stale, negative, and tired chi is flushed out. The drain on the life force of the house is arrested and a happy ambience is quickly established. And then it is a matter of maintaining the feel-good chi in the home.

Throughout the book are checklists designed to help you identify your home's energy robbers – you will see at a glance how, by simply opening a window or a door, or by moving a mirror, changing a ceiling, or buying a new carpet, you can safeguard the harmony of your home. And you will also learn to identify and demolish the hostile quarrelsome energies making everyone around you unhappy.

You will know at a glance where any illness chi lingers each year and from month to month, so you can suppress it. And most important, you will know how to put a stop to financial loss, broken relationships, frustrations, disharmony, and the pernicious effect of aggravating people. Also included are projects and question-and-answer boxes to guide you all the way.

When you invest the time and effort necessary to learn the living skill of feng shui, you will have added a valuable resource to your life – knowing how to enhance the space and time energy of your surroundings. As a result, your view of, and approach to, living spaces will never again be the same.

FIND YOUR CHINESE ASTROLOGY ANIMAL SIGN

RAT
31 Jan 1900 – 18 Feb 1901
18 Feb 1912 – 5 Feb 1913
5 Feb 1924 – 23 Jan 1925
24 Jan 1936 – 10 Feb 1937
10 Feb 1948 – 28 Jan 1949
28 Jan 1960 – 14 Feb 1961
15 Feb 1972 – 2 Feb 1973
2 Feb 1984 – 19 Feb 1985
19 Feb 1996 – 6 Feb 1997

OX
19 Feb 1901 – 7 Feb 1902
6 Feb 1913 – 25 Jan 1914
24 Jan 1925 – 12 Feb 1926
11 Feb 1937 – 30 Jan 1938
29 Jan 1949 – 16 Feb 1950
15 Feb 1961 – 4 feb 1962
3 Feb 1973 – 22 Jan 1974
20 Feb 1985 – 8 Feb 1986
7 Feb 1997 – 27 Jan 1998

TIGER
8 Feb 1902 – 28 Jan 1903
26 Jan 1914 – 13 Feb 1915
13 Feb 1926 – 1 Feb 1927
31 Jan 1938 – 18 Feb 1939
17 Feb 1950 – 5 Feb 1951
5 Feb 1962 – 24 Jan 1963
23 Jan 1974 – 10 Feb 1975
9 Feb 1986 – 28 Jan 1987
28 Jan 1998 – 15 Feb 1999

RABBIT
29 Jan 1903 – 15 Feb 1904
14 Feb 1915 – 2 Feb 1916
2 Feb 1927 – 22 Jan 1928
19 Feb 1939 – 7 Feb 1940
6 Feb 1951– 26 Jan 1952
25 Jan 1963 – 12 Feb 1964
11 Feb 1975 – 30 Jan 1976
29 Jan 1987 – 16 Feb 1998
1 Feb 1999 – 4 Feb 2000

DRAGON
16 Feb 1904 – 3 Feb 1905
3 Feb 1916 – 22 Jan 1917
23 Jan 1928 – 9 Feb 1929
8 Feb 1940 – 26 Jan 1941
27 Jan 1952 – 13 Feb 1953
13 Feb 1964 – 1 Feb 1965
31 Jan 1976 – 17 Feb 1977
17 Feb 1988 – 5 Feb 1989
5 Feb 2000 – 23 Jan 2001

SNAKE
4 Feb 1905 – 24 Jan 1906
23 Jan 1917 –10 Feb 1918
10 Feb 1929 – 29 Jan 1930
27 Jan 1941 – 14 Feb 1942
14 Feb 1953 – 2 Feb 1954
2 Feb 1965 – 20 Jan 1966
18 Feb 1977 – 6 Feb 1978
6 Feb 1989 – 26 Jan 1990
24 Jan 2001 – 11 Feb 2002

HORSE
25 Jan 1906 – 12 Feb 1907
11 Feb 1918 – 31 Jan 1919
30 Jan 1930 – 16 Feb 1931
15 Feb 1942 – 4 Feb 1943
3 Feb 1954 – 23 Jan 1955
21 Jan 1966 – 8 Feb 1967
7 Feb 1978 – 27 Jan 1979
27 Jan 1990 – 14 Feb 1991
12 Feb 2002 – 31 Jan 2003

SHEEP
13 Feb 1907 – 1 Feb 1908
1 Feb 1919 – 19 Feb 1920
17 Feb 1931 – 5 Feb 1932
5 Feb 1943 – 24 Jan 1944
24 Jan 1955 – 11 Fen 1956
9 Feb 1967   29 Jan 1968
28 Jan 1979 – 15 Feb 1980
15 Feb 1991 – 3 Feb 1992
1 Feb 2003 – 21 Jan 2004

MONKEY
2 Feb 1908 – 21 Jan 1909
20 Feb 1920 – 7 Feb 1921
6 Feb 1932 – 25 Jan 1933
25 Jan 1944 – 12 Feb 1945
12 Feb 1956 – 30 Jan 1957
30 Jan 1968 – 16 Feb 1969
16 Feb 1980 – 4 Feb 1981
4 Feb 1992 – 22 Jan 1993
22 Jan 2004 – 8 Feb 2005

ROOSTER
22 Jan 1909 – 9 Feb 1910
8 Feb 1921 – 27 Jan 1922
26 Jan 1933 – 13 Feb 1934
13 Feb 1945 – 1 Feb 1946
31 Jan 1957 – 17 Feb 1958
17 Feb 1969 – 5 Feb 1970
5 Feb 1981 – 24 Jan 1982
23 Jan 1993 – 9 Feb 1994
9 Feb 2005 – 28 Jan 2006

DOG
10 Feb 1910 – 29 Jan 1911
28 Jan 1922 – 15 Feb 1923
14 Feb 1934 – 3 Feb 1935.
2 Jan 1946 – 21 Jan 1947
18 Feb 1958 – 7 Feb 1959
6 Feb 1970 – 26 Jan 1971
25 Jan 1982 – 12 Feb 1983
10 Feb 1994 – 30 Jan 1995
29 Jan 2006 – 17 Feb 2007

BOAR
30 Jan 1911 – 17 Feb 1912
16 Feb 1923 – 4 Feb 1924
4 Feb 1935 – 23 Jan 1936
22 Jan 1947 – 9 Feb 1948
8 Feb 1959 – 27 Jan 1960
27 Jan 1971 – 14 Feb 1972
13 Feb 1983 – 1 Feb 1984
31 Jan 1995 – 18 Feb 1996
18 Fen 2007 – 6 Feb 2008

Part One

Feng Shui Afflictions Inside and Outside the Home

PHYSICAL FENG SHUI AFFLICTIONS

The first step in creating a happy home is to learn to be aware of all the physical afflictions that may exist there – afflictions that can cause all manner of misfortune, illness, and aggravation. Systematically identifying and remedying the physical things that are incorrectly placed or causing problems within rooms and on beds, desks, and tables will collectively go a long way in improving your overall feng shui. It is only after you have smoothed the flow of chi around you by facilitating its movement within your space that you will begin to feel the calming bliss of good energy. This happens when everything tangible around you emits embracing, rather than debilitating, chi.

Physical afflictions create bad spatial feng shui 1

Modern homes are designed with so many corners, pillars, levels, and shapes that, quite unknowingly, they could be creating secret "poison arrows". To become aware of the number of sharp, straight, and pointed features inside and outside your home, and the energy they create, all you need do is look around you. Unless your attention is drawn to these physically jarring features and their killing vibrations, it is surprisingly easy to miss them. But as soon as you become aware of the dynamics and influences they exert on your immediate physical environment, you will have taken the first step toward that ancient, yet still relevant, practice of feng shui.

What to look out for

Be aware of anything straight and long, such as a straight road aimed right at your front door (see also Tip 5), or a long internal corridor "hitting" the door to the master

Look out for feng shui afflictions around your home – such as pylons, trees, and the edges of nearby buildings that appear to "hit" your home.

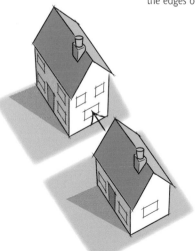

Rooflines of buildings in close proximity to your home can create external "poison arrows", or shar chi – negative energy that afflicts your living space. It is vital to check for environmental feng shui problems before you begin to address the feng shui within your home's interior.

bedroom. Also, note anything sharp, such as the edge of a nearby building directed at your house, or the edge of a pillar in the living room hitting the place you regularly sit. Equally, beware anything triangular in shape, such as the roof line of a neighbor's house aimed at your front door or one of your windows (see left), or an abstract painting hanging above your living-room fireplace that features sharp, triangular shapes. All of these environmental afflictions can create slivers of arrows hitting you, so now it's time to stop living with them – and take action. Read on to discover the feng shui remedies you'll need.

2   Furniture arrangements disturb your peace

Look at the arrangement of the furniture in the main rooms of your home. This may seem a minor point, but the way furniture is placed in living spaces has a direct bearing on the peace of your home. Beds, tables, and chairs all emanate energy that can sometimes produce a negative effect on anybody living there. Also, remember that the sleeping and sitting spaces will always interact with the personal chi energy of all the residents. Those of you who are familiar with the Kua formula of personalized auspicious and inauspicious directions based upon your birth year (see Tip 19) already know about the importance of auspicious sleeping and sitting directions.

In addition to the Kua formula of good and bad directions, it is also essential to observe the feng shui ground rules when it comes to placing significant pieces of furniture.

Balanced furniture placement and minimal clutter allows chi to flow freely throughout the room.

How to arrange your furniture at home

Foyers or halls
Nothing in the foyer or hall should block chi from entering the home. When good chi finds it hard to enter, the effect is a lack of vitality. The center of the front of the house is usually referred to as the "facing palace of the house," and it is very important to keep it auspicious and not afflicted by the presence of heavy pieces of furniture – perhaps have a single, auspicious screen to force the chi to meander around the screen as it enters the home. There should also, ideally, be a door or a window in the foyer or hall.

Living rooms
Sofas and coffee tables should never block the path of chi as it enters the home. Avoid confrontational arrangements, such as sofas positioned directly opposite each other, as this tends to encourage mental conflicts and arguments. A hexagonal or octagonal Pa Kua type arrangement (see below) is conducive to the creation of harmonious energy. Place small side tables next to sofa chairs – this makes for pleasant chi, as each person has his or her own aura of space, and reduces the potential for tension and hostility.

Dining rooms
Never place the dining table directly under a toilet on the floor above or directly next to a toilet. Dining tables should not appear cramped, so if the room is small use a wall mirror to extend the space visually. Try to assign seating places for every person around the table according to their individual *nien yen* or *fu wei* direction (see Tip 19). This is an excellent arrangement for producing harmony at meal times.

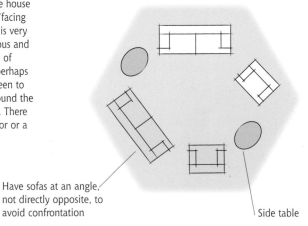

Have sofas at an angle, not directly opposite, to avoid confrontation

Side table

Doors bring aggravation   3

The main entrance door is considered to be the mouth of the home, where sustenance and good-fortune chi can enter. Many aspects of feng shui address the positioning and orientation of the door, as well as its color, size, and other attributes, which also have a bearing on how good it is for your home. Of all the guidelines to do with the door, the one with the most powerful influence on the well-being of residents is probably orientation.

Door orientation

It is always best that the main door face the same direction as the house. This brings harmony and balance to the energies surrounding the home. Even when it is not

The facing direction of your house usually matches the main door direction .

possible to have the main door located in this way, you should at least have a secondary door or a window there. This will usually act as a replacement entrance, or mouth.

A badly oriented door is one that is said to "fight" with the facing direction of the house. When this describes your main door, you are sure to suffer all manner of aggravations. Follow the table below and use the remedies suggested to reduce the ill-effects of a conflicting door.

Door remedies

FACING DIRECTION OF HOUSE	FACING DIRECTION OF DOOR AND ITS EFFECTS	REMEDY TO PLACE BY DOOR
House facing South (fire)	Door facing Southeast: produces	Do nothing
	Door facing Southwest: exhausts	Place metal
House facing North (water)	Door facing Northeast: destroys	Place plants
	Door facing Northwest: produces	Do nothing
House facing West (metal)	Door facing Southwest: produces	Do nothing
	Door facing Northwest: allies	Do nothing
House facing East (wood)	Door facing Northeast: destroys	Place water
	Door facing Southeast: allies	Do nothing
House facing Southwest (earth)	Door facing South: produces	Do nothing
	Door facing West: exhausts	Place water
House facing Northeast (earth)	Door facing North: distracts	Do nothing
	Door facing East: destroys	Place lights
House facing Southeast (wood)	Door facing East: allies	Do nothing
	Door facing South: exhausts	Place stones
House facing Northwest (metal)	Door facing North: exhausts	Place plants
	Door facing West: allies	Do nothing

For plant remedies, display plants with rounded leaves, such as a peace lily.

Note:
When a door "produces" or "allies", the effect on the residents is auspicious. Do nothing.

When a door "exhausts", the effect is inauspicious and requires remedies to be placed at the door.

When the door "distracts", the effect is neutral and nothing needs to be done

When the door "destroys", the effect is inauspicious and requires remedies to be placed at the door.

4 Castle-gate doors attract amazing good luck

One of the best-kept secrets of advanced feng shui practice, which, until recent years, was known only to serious practitioners in Asia, is to install a castle-gate door. This is a main door angled at about 45° to the facing direction of the house, or 45° to the line of the house. A castle-gate door cannot change the facing direction of a property, but it is one way to capture an auspicious personalized direction, based on the Kua formula, in the event that the facing direction of a home is not personally auspicious. The Kua formula identifies a person's auspicious and inauspicious directions based on their year of birth (see Tip 19). For example, if the house appears to be aligned alongside the road outside and is facing, say, South, while the direction that is auspicious for you is Southwest, then you can angle the door so that instead of facing South it faces Southwest. The door then becomes a castle-gate door.

A castle-gate door is tilted to around 45°.   Tilted door

A castle-gate door is one that is angled at 45°, and in the East is often used to harness a person's auspicious Kua direction when the facing direction of the house is unlucky.

Castle-gate doors in Singapore

There are many examples of castle-gate doors in Singapore where, for a number of years, the island's most prominent feng shui master used it with great success to benefit many local tycoons. Thus, along the famous Orchard Road, you can see examples of tilted doors at the front of numerous buildings.

The best-known example of the tilted door effect is that of the Grand Hyatt Hotel, located on Scotts Road in downtown Singapore. When this hotel first opened its doors in the 1960s, business was poor, so Ven. Hong Choon, the famous feng shui master, was asked for his help. He advised that the hotel install a tilted door, and when it was completed the hotel received a planeload of guests when a flight was suddenly delayed. From that day on, the Grand Hyatt has become one of the country's most successful hotels.

Many homes in Singapore and Malaysia today have the castle-gate effect in place to bring their owners amazing good fortune.

Afflicted main doors cause great misfortune 5

When the main door, or even a frequently used secondary door, into the home becomes afflicted by the impact of a poison arrow sending killing energy toward it, residents will have a great many things to worry about. Poison arrows are normally caused by structures or natural landforms found outside the house facing the main door (see Tip 1).

Door dangers

These physical afflictions can result from a straight road aimed at the door, a triangular roof line from across the road, an elevated roadway, or a single large tree, transmission tower, or bridge. Indeed, just about any type of structure that seems to overwhelm your door or which appears to be sending out hostile vibes can produce physical afflictions. The modern feng shui term coined to describe these afflictions is "secret poison arrows", and they are usually the principal causes of misfortune luck. They are, however, not difficult to identify.

Effective remedies

Dealing with these physical afflictions is not difficult when you know how. The secret is in discovering the source of the poison arrow – in other words, the direction from which it is coming. Knowing this enables you to put effective cures and remedies in place to intercept the poison arrow before it hits the house and its door. The best advice is to invest in a good compass and then, standing in front of your house facing outward, take the compass direction of the structure that represents the offending physical affliction. Once you have this information, note the following advice:

- If it is coming from the South, place a large urn of water near the door.

- If it is coming from the North, place a large boulder or crystal near the door.

Invest in a large water bowl or urn, as a water-filled urn represents yin energy and is a common cure for afflicted areas outside the home.

- If it is coming from the West and Northwest, place a bright light near the door.

- If it is coming from the East and Southeast, place windchimes near the door.

- If it is coming from the Northeast or Southwest, place plants near the door.

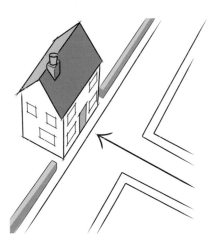

A T-junction creates a poison arrow directed at the front door – a common feng shui affliction.

6   Water to the right of the door causes infidelity

When placing feng shui water cures or enhancers, never position them on the right side of the door into your home – by either the main entrance or near any secondary door that is frequently used. The right side here refers to the right side when you are inside looking out.

Breaking the rule

The result of breaking this rule is that the man of the house will, at best, develop a roving eye and, at worst, he could even start a secret second family. This is a common consequence of ignoring this rule and it almost always results in heartbreak and tragedy when the man is eventually found out.

As long as this water-placement rule is observed, then the marriage of those living within the home will not be negatively affected. It applies to the placing of all water features, whether inside or outside the home. When water is placed directly in front of a door, however, it can act either as a cure or an enhancer. You will discover later in this book that there are certain orientations where the placement of water can be extremely auspicious, bringing wealth and higher income luck (see Tip 78).

Check your water features

Water placed at the front of the home to the right of the front door (see left) can cause unfaithfulness in relationships. Also, check that any back entrances to your home are not similarly afflicted (see below). Watch out for accidental water features, such as empty urns or discarded pots left by doors – if they fill with rain water, they act just like a decorative installation, causing infidelity.

A mirror reflecting the front door brings in hostility

7

The consequences of having a large wall mirror directly reflecting your entrance door are sickness and hostile competitive pressures from external malevolent parties. It also causes any projects, businesses, or career progress to become bogged down by the many obstacles that seem to block your path to success. Some people say that the mirror causes chi to fly in and then instantly out of your home, especially if the surface reflects the road outside. If the wall mirror is by the side of the foyer or entrance hall and does not directly reflect the door, it does no harm.

The danger of too much yang

If the mirror reflects a high wall at the front of the house, it is also acceptable. However, ensure that when the front door opens the mirror does not reflect outside yang energy, such as main roads, stores, or markets. The idea is to make certain that any chi that enters your home is not quickly sucked out again. Placing a screen in front of the door to block the mirror is also an acceptable remedy.

Where to hang mirrors

If your mirror is opposite your main door, but you have a high gate or boundary wall that is reflected in the mirror, this is not inauspicious (see right, above). However, if you can move your hall mirror it is preferable to hang it to the side of the main door (see right, below).

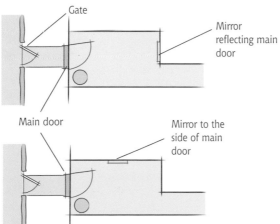

Gate

Mirror reflecting main door

Main door

Mirror to the side of main door

A mirror that directly faces an entrance causes chi energy to dissipate before it can benefit you. The staircase shown here directly facing the door is also not a good feature – correct it by having a bright light in the entrance hall.

8 Mirrors facing the bed bring a third party into the marriage

If you want your home to be happy and joyous, it is crucial to use feng shui to ensure the sanctity of your marriage, or the marriage of anybody living under your roof. Fidelity between partners should be a major goal of your feng shui efforts, as there is nothing more heartbreaking and damaging to the happiness of a home than the breakdown of a relationship caused by the intrusion of a third party or by indiscretions committed by either of the marriage partners.

Q & A

Q: *I can't move my bedroom mirror, so what else can I do?*

A: If your bedroom mirror is fixed to a wall or to the inside of a closet and cannot easily be moved, the best way to cope is to find a way of "closing" it so that it does not reflect the bed. Try using a decorative screen, wall hanging, or curtain. Blocking the mirror from view when you sleep is often sufficient to counteract the unlucky influences of bedroom mirrors.

To protect your relationship, keep your bedroom free of mirrors and harsh lighting.

Prevention is better than cure

One of the most common causes of a marriage breaking down is having a large reflective surface, such as a mirror, directly reflecting the marital bed. This reflection introduces a third-party outsider to come between husband and wife. Don't wait until this affliction causes you or your partner to stray from the marriage or to move out of the home altogether, for then it will be too late to do much.

In feng shui, remember that prevention is always better than cure, so remove all mirrors from the bedroom. It is better to dress and put on your make-up in the bathroom or designate another room or annex for this purpose. Take note that a television or a computer monitor facing the bed also counts as a reflective surface.

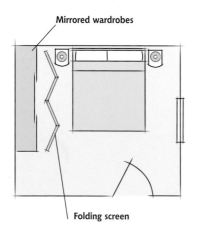

Mirrored wardrobes

Folding screen

If you have mirrored closets that you cannot get rid of, cover the mirrors with a lightweight folding screen before you go to bed. Mirrors create excess yang energy in a bedroom, which should always be a peaceful, yin space conducive to sleep.

Long corridors cause problems with siblings 9

One of the most common causes of fighting and quarrling between brothers and sisters is due to bedroom location – when siblings' bedroom doors all open onto a long corridor. When this unfortunate arrangement occurs, too many "mouths" are created by the doors leading onto the corridor. Long, narrow halls are usually frowned on in feng shui, unless they are part of an outdoor veranda surrounding the house. When located inside the house, the longer and narrower the corridor is, the more harmful it becomes – especially when there are rooms off it as well as a room at the very end. People living in rooms opening onto such a corridor are likely to harbor animosity toward each other, especially those whose doors directly face each other in a confrontational manner.

Introducing distractions

As you are unlikely to be able to change the arrangement of doors, the cure for this situation is to create distractions in the corridor. You can do this by hanging art on the walls and introducing potted plants (if space allows), since this will cause the flow of chi to slow down. This is the correct way to transform chi from hostile to benevolent. When chi moves too fast, it is negative and harmful, bringing with it misfortune and bad luck.

Too many doors

Lots of doors leading off a hall or long corridor represent many mouths. In the case of siblings, this layout symbolizes everyone talking at once, leading to quarrels and disagreements. Use plants here to create some peace and quiet – they act to slow down overactive yang chi.

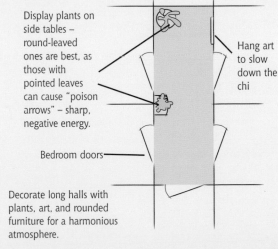

Display plants on side tables – round-leaved ones are best, as those with pointed leaves can cause "poison arrows" – sharp, negative energy.

Hang art to slow down the chi

Bedroom doors

Decorate long halls with plants, art, and rounded furniture for a harmonious atmosphere.

10 Confronting rooms lead to misunderstandings

When doors into bedrooms directly confront each other, there is certain to be misunderstandings between the occupants. This is one of the causes of sibling rivalry within families (see Tip 9). When daughters occupy rooms directly opposite each other, for example, the energy created will be one of hostile competition. This is particularly the case when one room door faces Southwest and the other faces Northeast – two earth chi directions confronting each other sets up a situation of intense rivalry.

Calming sibling rivalry

The cure for this situation is to install a bright light between the two doors. The light creates fire energy, which enhances the doors. Once there is sufficient resource chi created, the hostility evaporates. Bright lights also create precious yang energy, which is effective when the doors face other directions as well.

If sisters' bedroom doors are opposite one another, this can create intense sibling rivalry. Enhancing the hall with side tables and soft lighting can help calm hostile energy between the rooms.

Protruding corners cause temper tantrums   11

Some of the most common harmful afflictions found inside the home are protruding corners, which create sharp, knife-like edges. The effect of these corners is aggravating and usually causes people living in the house to lose their cool and become more quick-tempered than usual. Protruding corners also slice through relationships within the home. Anybody who happens to be sitting directly in the path of an edge will found that they are more susceptible than usual to all manner of stress, becoming easily provoked and having a low tolerance level.

Countermeasures

This particular affliction breaks up the peace of the household, and voices tend to become raised in anger and frustration. The way to overcome the problem is to place something in front of the knife like edge to block its killing energy. This could be a plant, a screen, a high closet, or a cupboard. To make your countermeasures more effective, you can also factor in the principle of the five elements, fine-tuning the remedy according to the direction in which the protruding edge is pointing.

So:

• When the edge is pointing to the South, its source is North; plants or crystals placed in front of the edge would be effective in nullifying its effect.

• When the edge is pointing to the North, its source is South; crystals or an urn of water placed in front of the protruding edge would be effective.

• When the edge is pointing to the Southwest its source is Northeast, and when Northeast the source is Sourthwest; place plants or windchimes in front of the protruding edge.

• When the edge is pointing to the East or Southeast, its source is Northwest or West; an urn of water or a bright light placed directly in front of the protruding edge will negate the affliction.

• When the edge points Northwest or West, the source is Southeast or East; either an urn of water or a bright light placed in front of the protruding edge would be effective.

Many modern homes have "poison arrow" pillars – the sharp corners that project negative chi and cause tempers to fray. Place round-leaved plants at the foot of these pillars to slow down the energy here and promote a more harmonious atmosphere.

12 Overhead beams make your head spin with pain

It is impossible to have balanced energy in any room where there are exposed overhead beams sending killing energy downward from the ceiling. If they are structural beams, their potency increases and the negative effect they have becomes even more intense. Overhead beams in massive apartment buildings are even more harmful. The remedy in these situations is to cover the beams completely, hiding them from sight. In feng shui, what is not seen and hidden from view generally loses most of its potency.

It is useful to note that overhead beams that are a part of a ceiling pattern are less harmful than a single, structural beam cutting across the room. However, when the home lacks a ceiling and the crossbeams as well as the roof tiles are visible, the effect is also negative. Friends who visit your home turn sour and friendships become spoiled due to misunderstandings and dis-agreements that tend to multiply, instead of getting

Overhead beams, particularly over the bed, can cause conflict in relationships. If you cannot move the bed away from the beams, cover them with fine fabric such as muslin to protect your relationship from this negative influence.

better, with time. Meanwhile, you and your spouse will have incessant fights and the house will be far from happy or calm. The remedy is to install a ceiling, pronto.

13 Water under the stairs turns children into brats

A bamboo ornament will make children far less rebellious.

This is one of the worst features you can have in your home, as it is said to make any children living there endure misfortune. Water under the staircase, such as a toilet, fishtank, or miniature fountain, also causes them to become somewhat less than adorable – and transforms them into disobedient, rebel-lious brats. Water under the staircase will also bring long-term bad luck to the sons of the family. Whatever project or educational work they are involved in will suffer from unex-pected setbacks, and they will meet with obstacles and troublemakers during their life.

Cures and talismans

It is best to stop using a toilet under the stair-case, but as this is rarely practical, just keep the toilet door closed. Remove water features immediately and place a ceramic or gold pagoda in the vicinity of the staircase. The pagoda has a powerful, positive effect on growing children. In the old days, parents would even have their children wear a pagoda pendant to attract good study chi. You can also place an old jade or ceramic decorative bamboo plant in children's bedrooms to aid their concentration.

Staircase blues create miscommunication 14

There are different types of staircase, each one creating a unique flow of chi energy as it moves upward to the next level of the home. Take the following points into account when installing a staircase:

- The best staircase design is wide and curving, ideally wide enough for two people to pass.

- The staircase should look solid and not be open with holes between the stair risers.

- The staircase should not start or end directly facing a door, and especially not the main front entrance.

- A staircase should not appear to be "split" when it is near the main door – in other words, with a flight of steps going up and another flight of steps going down. This confuses the chi entering the home.

Staircases should turn softly and be decorated with airy, simple furnishings and art. Always keep the area well lit.

When staircases go around and around, as in a spiral, or have many twists and turns, the effect is like a corkscrew causing the flow of chi to become staccato and abrupt.

The flow of chi

Ignoring any of these staircase design features will cause constant misunderstandings between people living in the house. This is because staircases are major conduits of chi, and the more harmonious and gently curving they are, the more benevolent will be the flow of chi. If you have the staircase blues, the cure is to place paintings along the walls that go up the stairway and to install a very bright light guiding the chi gently upward.

The reason so much attention is focused on having good feng shui staircases is that they conduct chi from one level of the home to the next, and if you hope to enjoy harmonious energy, day and night, then staircase energy must be right.

15 A window behind your bed makes you short-tempered

One of the most common sleeping taboos found in bedrooms is placing the head of a bed against a wall with a window in it. This means that the window will be behind the bed, which is an arrangement that signifies bad feng shui. A window behind the bed makes the sleeping person very vulnerable to yin spirit formations. This disturbs the sleep and, in turn, make the person very short-tempered and grumpy. This arrangement of bed and window is also responsible for giving the occupants disturbing dreams when they finally do manage to get to sleep.

Blocking outside chi

The cure for this problem is simple. At night when you are sleeping, close the window and draw heavy curtains across it to prevent outside chi from entering the bedroom. It is also an excellent idea to place a five-element pagoda on the window ledge as a protective symbol.

If in capturing your best sleeping direction you have to place your bed in front of a window, then all you need to do is ensure you have a thick curtain to close off the window while you sleep.

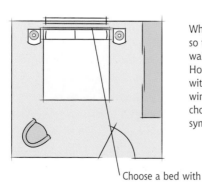

Choose a bed with a solid headboard.

Whever possible, angle your bed so that the bed head is against a wall rather than under a window. However, if you have to sleep with your bed positioned under a window, hang heavy curtains and choose a solid headboard to symbolize support.

A bedroom television disrupts relationships   16

The television screen is like a mirror and if it directly faces the bed, it could cause the couple marital disharmony (see Tip 8). The television also emits energy that could simply be too strong for the bedroom. If you are one of the many people who want a television in the bedroom, then make sure that it is covered with a cloth or closed off in a cabinet when you sleep. And definitely make certain that the screen is not facing Southwest. The best place to put the television is in the Northwest of the bedroom facing Southeast. In this orientation it does the least harm to the relationship between the sleeping partners.

If you can't live without a television in your bedroom – or if you live in a bedsit or studio apartment – place the television in the Northwest of the room.

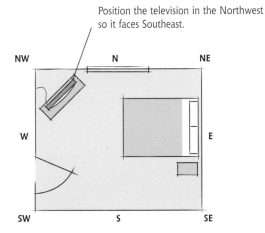

Position the television in the Northwest so it faces Southeast.

Q & A

Q: *How can I make my bedroom more yin? I can't stop my partner using the laptop in the bedroom.*

A: It is not so much a question of making your bedroom more yin as making it less yang. Keep the bedroom quiet, and decorate it in restful colors. Go for darker tones as opposed to brighter pastel shades and introduce soft, warm lighting.

17   Toilets deplete your luck

Toilets are best when they are small and unobtrusive. This is because toilets afflict the luck of the corners they occupy, often causing marital unhappiness and wealth luck to be flushed away. In truth, there is no place that is "right" for a toilet in the home. In the old days, the homes of the wealthy had no toilets – these were brought in and cleaned daily. Even baths were brought in and then taken away. And in the homes of the less well-off, toilets were built a little away from the main house.

Using element cures

In modern homes, the best way to ensure that toilets do not cause bad luck of any kind is not to enhance the chi inside toilets – so small bathrooms are ideal. This way they occupy only a small part of lucky corners. Next, systematically neutralize the afflicted chi energy within all the toilets of your home using element cures. The cures are simple, and they

are aimed at exhausting the chi energy inside the toilets. Begin by using a compass to find the orientation of all the toilets in your home.

Check out your bathroom's location and its element remedy.

- Place earth energy inside toilets located in the South – for example, an empty ceramic vase. Have an ochre color scheme.

- Place wood energy inside toilets in the North by introducing some healthy plants.

- Place water energy inside toilets located in the West and Northwest – for example, a water feature. Have a blue color scheme.

- Place fire energy inside toilets in the East or Southeast – have red tiles, display a red glitter lamp, and keep the room well lit.

- Place metal energy inside toilets located in the Southwest or Northeast – for example, a curved knife. Have white décor.

PROJECT

Fire symbolism

To bring the element of fire into a bathroom located in the Southeast or East, you will need a red item, the color of fire. You can also use anything that is both red and triangular, as the triangle is the associated element shape. A red glitter lamp adds extra yang energy as the glitter constantly moves.

Round dining tables result in harmonious meals 18

When it comes to selecting an auspicious dining table, it is useful to know that according to feng shui all the regular shapes are auspicious – square, rectangular, round, and even the octagonal Pa Kua shape. Each of the basic shapes also signify one of the five Chinese elements, and it is the square (Earth), rectangular (Wood) and the round (Metal) shapes that are best for dining tables. The Fire element shape is triangular, while the Water shape is wavy.

The harmonious circle

The Chinese have always had a preference for round dining tables, because this is the shape that make for harmonious meals. Family members quarrel and disagree less when the table is curved. A round table also has no sharp edges to disturb the harmony of the home. Indeed, it is rare to find anything but a round table in the dining rooms of Chinese homes – and the larger the table, the more auspicious it is deemed to be. In addition, these tables are almost always made of the finest woods and are either carved with a

A circular dining table symbolizes heaven chi and harmonious relationships.

collection of auspicious symbols or engraved with four-season fruits, plants, or flowers signifying auspicious abundance throughout the entire year.

The circle is also a special symbol signifying heaven chi. There is, thus, less possibility of energy becoming aggravating and the authority of the father figure is respected. Family members who sit together at a round table are deemed to be connected within a good relationship. To ensure good feng shui, individually and collectively, everyone should be allocated a seat around the table according to his/her best direction. Use the Kua formula of personalized good and best directions (see Tip 19) to maximize their luck each time they sit down to dine together. Select the nien yen, or family direction, for each person living in the house.

What's the element of your table?

A rectangular table symbolizes the Wood element.

A square table symbolizes the element of Earth.

A round table signifies Metal, the most auspicious feng shui table shape.

19   Sit in your nien yen direction for family harmony

Sit facing your nien yen direction for more family unity.

Find your nien yen direction

YOUR KUA NUMBER	YOUR NIEN YEN DIRECTION	EAST OR WEST GROUP?
1	South	East
2	Northwest	West
3	Southeast	East
4	East	East
5 *		West
6	Southwest	West
7	Northeast	West
8	West	West
9	North	East

* Those with Kua number 5: women read Kua 8, men read Kua number 2.

Sitting directions can create relationship woes when they are oriented to harm rather than benefit individuals. If you want to make the best of compass-formula feng shui to create happy, harmonious energy for everyone in the home, it is an excellent idea to learn the Kua formula. Once you have calculated your Kua number, you can determine your personalized family orientation. This is your nien yen direction. Facing this direction when you sit will bring harmony in all your relationships. It also ensures that the family unit stays happy and intact. Set a place for each family member around the dining table so that they each face their nien yen. Calculate your Kua number and determine your nien yen direction as follows:

Calculating your Kua number

Everyone's personal auspicious and inauspicious directions are based on gender and date of birth, and from these basic details you can calculate your Kua number. There are 9 Kua numbers altogether, each belonging to either the East or West group of directions. To find out your Kua number, follow these steps:

1 Take the last two digits of your year of birth and add them together until the result is a single digit. However, if you are born in January you need to make an adjustment for the lunar year and deduct one year from your year of birth before applying the formula.

2 Next, if you are male, deduct the number obtained from 10 and the result is your Kua number. If you are female, add 5 to the number to find your Kua number.

3 Reduce this number to a single digit if necessary.

Example: for a female born in 1970:
$7 + 0 = 7$; females add 5, so $7 + 5 = 12$;
$1 + 2 = 3$, so the Kua number is 3.

Toilets near the front door bring a host of problems 20

If you have a toilet situated near the main front door – either immediately facing it or positioned on the next floor directly above the front door, so that it presses down upon it – good luck flies out of the home. This can make the family terribly unhappy, as there will be misunderstandings between the parents and between parents and children. They simply cannot live in peace and health when these afflictions make their presence felt. And when the chi energy of the year and month are harmful (see Tip 43) the afflictions become compounded and the situation deteriorates still further.

Toilet remedies

The remedy for a badly located toilet is to keep the toilet door closed at all times. Toilets located above the main door bring severe bad luck to the entire household and therefore, to counter the negative effects, you need to shine a very bright light up at the ceiling to symbolically lift the chi. However, if the affliction proves to be too excessive or severe, you might have no option other than to relocate the toilet

The location of a downstairs bathroom impacts upon the luck of your house.

Toilet afflictions

Toilets that directly face the door cause all energy entering the home to become negative. And, depending on the direction of the toilet vis-à-vis the main front door, the toilet can affect different kinds of luck as follows:

• Wealth luck is afflicted when the toilet is Southeast of the door.
• Career luck is disturbed when the toilet is North of the door.
• Romance and love luck becomes non-existent when the toilet is Southwest of the door.
• Descendants luck is hurt when the toilet is West of the door.
• Patron luck is hard to come by when the toilet is Northwest of the door.
• The luck of the father is affected badly when the toilet is Northwest of the door.
• The luck of the mother is badly hurt when the toilet is Southwest of the door.

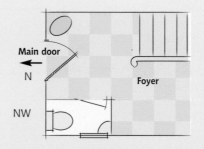

This toilet is located Northwest of the main door, which means you can have a hard time attracting patrons such as business investors or mentors.

• The health luck of residents is afflicted when the toilet is East of the door.
• The good name of the family is affected negatively when the toilet is South of the door.
• Study luck of the children is affected when the toilet is Northeast of the door.

21 Toilets in other parts of the home bring problems too

- **North** Toilets located in the North sector of the home causes problems with colleagues at work and with your bosses. It also creates blocks and places obstacles in the path of career advancement. The cure is to place a large stone inside the toilet room. Keep the door closed at all times and do not decorate the room in blue or black.

- **South** Toilets placed in the South sector of the home cause gossip and backbiting. People living in the home will become victims of slander and the good name of the family will be compromised. The cure is to place an urn of water inside the bathroom and keep the lights in the toilet dim.

- **East** Toilets placed here cause the sons of the family to become rebellious. If the family is childless, the chances of conceiving a son will be spoiled by a toilet here. The health of residents will also be affected. The cure is to place bright lights inside the toilet.

- **West** Toilets placed in the West sector of the home will bring problems for the children of the house. If you are childless, you will also find that your descendants luck is afflicted, so conceiving a child becomes

When checking your bathroom location, check the sector that the entire bathroom occupies, not just the toilet area.

difficult. The cure is to place a painting of water, such as a lake or waterfall, in the toilet.

- **Southwest** Toilets placed in the Southwest sector of the home will have a negative effect on the marriage prospects of any eligible children in the home. It will also affect the relationship between husband and wife. Place flowers and plants inside the toilet. Do not place crystals or ceramic pots there.

- **Northeast** Toilets placed in the Northeast sector affect children's concentration, making it hard for them to study at home. The cure is to place plants in the toilet to overcome the bad energy being created. Decorate the room in green tiles.

- **Southeast** Toilets placed in the Southeast sector of the home cause financial loss, a slowdown of business, and a fall in profits. There will always seem to be a shortage of cash. The cure is to hang a five-rod pagoda windchime or a curved knife in the room. Use white tiles to decorate.

- **Northwest** Toilets placed in the Northwest sector of the home hurt the father figure and affect all networking luck. Everybody living in the house will find it hard to forge ahead. The cure is to install bright lights and keep them turned on for at least three hours a day to obliterate the bad effects.

A five-rod pagoda windchime protects against financial loss caused by a toilet in the Southeast.

Kitchens to the right of the front door cause family friction

22

Another feng shui affliction that causes family members to become embroiled in bitter battles with each other occurs when the kitchen is located to the right (as you walk into the house) of the front door. The chi energy that builds up over time can cause severe family feuds, especially if the family is wealthy and there are assets to be divided among the children. There will be fights over any inheritance and, even if the parents are alive, there will still be much quarrelling.

The dangers of northwest kitchens

Kitchens should also not be placed in the Northwest sector of the house, as this can cause severe misfortunes and financial losses for the head of the family. Sometimes a kitchen in the Northwest sector can even cause the house to catch fire.

Kitchens in the Northwest or to the right of the main door can cause conflict over money.

Kitchen locations must be determined with great care, as a badly-located kitchen is one of the hardest feng shui problems to overcome. Placing an urn of still water might help, but it is only a temporary measure.

Q & A

Q: *I live in a rented apartment and my kitchen is in the Northwest. Do I have to move?*

A: No. Try to move the stove or oven away from the Northwest corner of the kitchen – the idea is not to have fire energy, represented by the oven, in the Northwest corner. If you really cannot do this, place an urn of yin (still) water next to the stove.

33

23 Repair blocks in your home for success

House maintenance guards against bad feng shui. One of the most crucial activities that you need do each year is systematically to identify all the implements and utilities that need to be repaired, changed, or upgraded. So, repair all leaking or rusty pipes; change electrical sockets that are worn out; remove all unnecessary nails in walls around the home; fill any holes in walls caused by removing nails; and trim all trees and shrubs around the garden and get rid of overgrown creepers and grass. Those living in hot climates should be extra careful of trees such as the banyan, whose roots can burrow deep into your home's foundations, causing distress to the building without you being aware of it.

Refresh your home's chi

All plumbing and electrical wiring that has become faulty or is broken must be repaired immediately for safety reasons, and in feng shui terms because they create blocks to success and cause aggravation and disputes among family members. If you want your home to be happy and peaceful, and if you want the energy to flow, keep the chi fresh at all times.

In the same vein, throw out any broken or chipped glasses. Damaged decorative urns, vases, and even art should be thrown out, restored, or tucked away in the attic. Displaying anything at all that is flawed or broken is an extremely bad idea.

Don't hang on to chipped glass or crockery, and have leaks and blockages fixed to avoid the accumulation of stuck, negative chi that can disrupt family relationships.

Afflictions are caused by intangible bad chi   24

Knowing about physical feng shui really is only half the picture. To be truly effective you need to go beyond repairing the physical problems of feng shui within your home. This brings us to the realm of the changing energy patterns that affect us, and these are caused by intangible forces. These forces are explained in the different formulas of feng shui, which enable us to draw up luck maps and feng shui charts of houses.

These charts reveal secrets that point the way for us to make good luck better and bad luck bearable. The secrets of the feng shui charts have, in recent years, amazed a growing number of people through their sheer effectiveness. Many are discovering that just about anyone can learn to understand feng shui charts and use the relevant ones to improve their prospects and enjoy a happier lifestyle.

In feng shui, energy moves around the world in 20-year cycles, or periods.

Cyclical movements of energy

Different feng shui charts reveal the way energy is distributed in the various sectors of the home from one period to the next. This energy is the invisible chi that brings both good luck and misfortune, and it does so in a cyclical way. This invisible chi energy is constantly transforming from good to bad and to good again over periods of time – periods of time that are expressed as months, as years, and as 20-year periods. Think of them as cyclical movements of energy that are continuously and simultaneously rotating. Thus, in any moment of time, different daily, monthly, yearly, and period cyclical energies are coming together to create patterns and concentrations of good and bad luck. So afflictions – illness, loss of income, accidents, job obstacles, and all other types of misfortune – can manifest into physical space caused by nothing more than the passage of time. When you know how to identify these cyclical causes of bad luck and learn how to overcome their pernicious effects, you will be maximizing your use of feng shui.

A change to the time period also influences the collective unconscious of the world's peoples. So in the preceding period of 7 the pursuit of wealth was a priority, whereas in the current period of 8 you will find that people become more introspective, pursuing relationships and health issues more keenly. This is because period 8 is ruled by the trigram Ken, representing the mountain, which traditionally symbolizes health and relationship energies.

As time passes, the world's chi energy changes, which impacts upon the luck of your home.

25   Weak energy creates the negative syndrome

The key to using feng shui charts is to learn to differentiate between the different types of harmful energy. Thus there is a difference between chi energy that is weak and chi energy that is killing. Obviously, weak energy is not nearly as harmful as killing energy – nevertheless it does cause illness and aggravation to those living in your home. Compass formula offers methods of identifying the corners of the house that suffer from weak energy through a system of codes using numbers to reveal the state of the energy. The numbers 1 to 9 each represent different types of energies – good as well as bad. In addition, there are also combinations of numbers that are allocated to different sectors of the house, and these offer yet more information on the chi energy of the sectors.

It is not difficult to learn to read the feng shui charts and luck maps created by the different formulas. If you follow these tips step by step, you will soon be able to identify which feng shui chart and luck map that apply to your home.

Nuances of energy

Before going into the chart itself, it is useful to understand the nuances of energy. Thus it is useful to bear in mind that weak energy creates a vulnerability to illness, small accidents, and a lack of strength. You will feel lethargic and constantly tired, but remember that weak energy is not brought by physical structures in your home, but simply by the passing of time.

So it is necessary to identify the parts of your home that have weak energy in any year or in any month. Once you identify the place of weak chi it is easy enough to strengthen it using the five-element therapy cures. To detect weak energy in the home, use the compass formula – the annual flying star affliction chart (see Tip 43).

A home that has positive, balanced chi rarely witnesses the minor accidents caused by weak energy.

Dead energy creates the failure syndrome 26

Dead energy brings growth awareness to a dead stop. It is usually identified as the sector of the home that is afflicted by the bad luck chi energy, described under the eight mansions Kua formula of feng shui (see Tip 19). Under this method of compass formula feng shui, there are eight types of house and this categorization is based on the home's facing direction, from which eight-mansion luck maps can be drawn. There are, therefore, eight types of luck map, and the location of the sector that tends to have "dead energy" is summarized in the table opposite. Use the table to identify this sector in your home, and then apply the suggested method to transform the sector's chi energy so that it comes alive to benefit people in that sector.

Detect your home's "dead energy" sector

HOUSE FACING DIRECTION	SECTOR WHERE ENERGY IS DEAD	BEST WAY TO TRANSFORM ENERGY OF SECTOR
Southeast	West	Not necessary to do anything
South	Southwest	Place a large plant in the Southwest
Southwest	South	Place urn of water in the South
East	Northeast	Place a large plant in the Northeast
West	Southeast	Not necessary to do anything
Northeast	East	Not necessary to do anything
North	Northwest	Not necessary to do anything
Northwest	North	Place a large plant in the Northeast

Using the light cure

If the sector is "missing", due to the shape of the home, then the dead energy is outside the home, in which case placing a shining light in that missing corner will be beneficial. This is not as crucial as if the afflicted sector were inside the home.

Transforming the dead energy

Unless the dead energy is transformed, residents living in the affected sector of the home will suffer from the failure syndrome. Whatever they attempt to do they will find it hard to succeed. Dead energy deprives them of strength. Make an effort, therefore, to identify the place of intangible dead chi based on the table above.

Note, however, that if under other formulas of feng shui the sector afflicted by dead energy has good flying stars, for instance, then the stars effectively transform the energy from bad to good. If the stars bring bad energy, however, then the negativity is substantially increased.

Lighting up a missing Northeast corner

This L-shaped home has a missing Northeast sector. You can compensate for the dead energy created by the missing sector by placing a bright light outside as shown.

SE   S   SW

E   W

Door to patio area

NE   N   NW

Bright light placed outside in "dead energy" sector.

27 Killing energy causes accidents and misfortunes

Not surprisingly, intangible chi energy that is killing can often be very harmful, and unless you are aware of this affliction in the affected part of the house you will not know the reason for the misfortunes of those living there. Killing energy brings severe misfortunes that can, sometimes, even prove fatal. In many homes, the killing energy is neutralized without residents ever being aware of it because, when you look at the indicated method to "transform" the killing energy, the technique is really not that difficult.

However, if you consciously know what to do, results will be a lot less hit-and-miss and your life will be a lot more restful. So, using the chart below, check the facing direction of your house and then look in the third column to see what you need to do to neutralize the killing energy in the afflicted sector.

Placing a bright light as a cure for killing energy can be functional rather than just decorative.

Detect your home's "killing energy" sector

HOUSE FACING DIRECTION	LOCATION OF "KILLING ENERGY"	BEST WAY TO TRANSFORM THE ENERGY OF THE SECTOR
Southeast	Southwest	Place an urn of water in the sector
South	West	Place a bright light in the sector
Southwest	Southeast	Place a bright light in the sector
East	Northwest	Place a bright light in the sector
West	South	Don't do anything
Northeast	North	Don't do anything
North	Northeast	Place an urn of water in the sector
Northwest	East	Place a bright light in the sector

Negative energy requires a bright light   28

All negative energy needs to be revitalized, transformed, or, at the very least, kept under control. When the chi energy is severe and active, transforming its nature is the best way to deal with it. But when negative energy is stagnant, it needs to be revitalized. The two methods used to achieve this are not too different, and if you are not sure if the sector of the house where your room is located feels devoid of good, vibrant energy, then the best safeguard is always to introduce yang energy by installing a bright light.

Play safe

Shining a bright light in any corner will do wonders for the space, almost irrespective of the type of negative energy there. I nearly always keep at least one light turned on in every level of my home. At night, when chi energy turns yin, it is extremely beneficial to counter it with a bright light. So, if you find it difficult to remember which corner of your home requires remedies against negative chi, it is a good idea to use the effective cure-all of keeping a light turned on. Note that in feng shui lights signify yang energy, so ensuring the presence of yang energy during the night-time hours creates good balance in the home.

Always keep your home well-lit, particularly at night, to protect against negative energy.

PROJECT

Feng shui lighting

Round-based table lamps
A round-based lamp is excellent because the shape denotes an endless cycle of good luck. Choose a red colored base as an auspicious yang color.

Office-style desk lamps
Anglepoise-style lamps can look unfriendly! Choose a desk lamp that has a broad shade, which casts a larger pool of llight – this symbolically welcomes in good chi.

Spotlights
Spotlights are extremely helpful when they shine directly at the South wall of a room. However, be very careful that your spotlights are not too strong, or they create excessive energy. Remember, feng shui strives for balance.

Crystal chandeliers
This is one of the few all-round excellent feng shui energizers. The crystals in the chandelier reflect the light, bringing in added glow and warmth. Hang one in the South corner of any room to boost your fame potential.

29   Move your furniture to re-energize the home

In addition to using lights (see Tip 28), there are other ways to re-energize homes that may, for whatever reason, feel stagnant and tired. If you suspect that something is not quite right with the chi energy of a room, or even the whole house, the best way to deal with it is to revitalize the energy before trying to find out why the home feels that way. It is important to realize that while learning and using feng shui as a living skill is something beneficial, it is equally important to use your common sense, to trust your own instincts, and to give your home space a quick-fix before trying to find out what exactly may be wrong.

Moving the energy

Diagnostic feng shui can take time so, in the meantime, go ahead and re-energize the energy of your space. Do this by moving the energy – simply open the doors and windows, shake out the carpets and curtains, and shift all the furniture from its usual place by about 18 in (45 cm). This forces the energy of the space to shift. In addition, turn on all the lights, switch on the fans if your have them, and, if you wish to do so, treat some of the walls to a fresh coat of paint.

Clutter-clearing

Implicit in this re-energizing exercise is a clearing out of unwanted things and the cleansing of accumulated dirt and clutter – so re-energizing the home is both visible and physical. When undertaking this exercise, you will feel the energy of the space receive a lift – this is because you will be getting rid of stale energy and giving the surfaces of your home new energy. This quick-fix is, of course, temporary, but it will bring in fresh yang energy, lifting your spirits and your space.

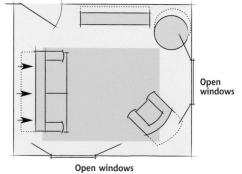

Give your home an energy boost by moving all the furnishings at least 18 in (45 cm) from their original positions, and open the windows.

Open windows

Open windows

The Lo Pan compass identifies intangible energy 30

Take the time to study ways in which to detect good and bad intangible energy in your living space. This is a skill worth acquiring and involves using a compass – the methods used to map out the luck sectors of homes are expressed as compass directions, so it really is impossible to go very deeply into the subject without using the compass to obtain your bearings. There is a special need for accuracy here, as feng shui does not stop at dividing orientations into just eight directions. On the Lo Pan compass used by feng shui practitioners, each direction is divided into three sub-directions, giving a total of 24.

Q & A

Q: What are the 24 mountains of the compass?

A: The 24 mountains is the collective name for the 24 sub-directions of the compass. Feng shui flying star charts are drawn up on the basis of these 24 directions, or "mountains", each of which take up 15 degrees of compass space. The chi energy is different for each one, depending upon the age and facing direction of the house.

The Lo Pan compass

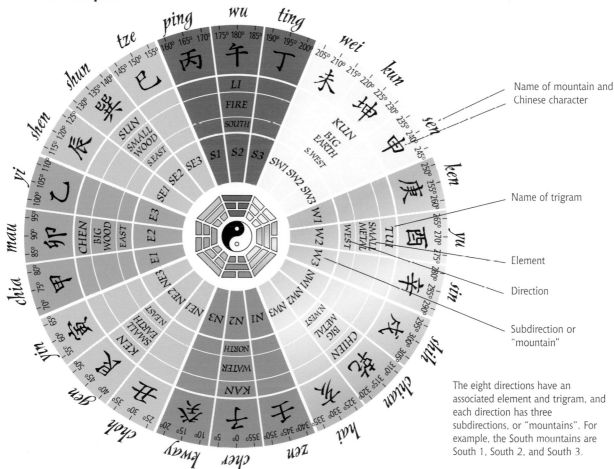

Name of mountain and Chinese character

Name of trigram

Element

Direction

Subdirection or "mountain"

The eight directions have an associated element and trigram, and each direction has three subdirections, or "mountains". For example, the South mountains are South 1, South 2, and South 3.

31 Learn flying star feng shui

The fundamentals of flying star feng shui are the compass direction of your home, which gives its facing direction, and the associated flying star natal chart (shown below).

The door in the top center square indicates the facing direction of your home, so you can stand inside your main door pointing the chart toward it for easy orientation.

This compass formula method adds the extra dimensions of time and periods to the practice of feng shui. It enables you to identify the different types of intangible energies that constantly impact on the health and luck of physical structures – homes or other buildings. Learning flying star adds a new perspective to the practice of feng shui and, because it is technical in its approach, it is also easier to learn and to teach.

Using the charts

Flying star feng shui addresses chi energy by studying charts that are essentially based on the age of the building and its facing direction. The key is to identify the correct flying star chart that applies to the house you are analyzing. The method requires the analysis of the numbers in the nine sectors of that particular chart. By superimposing the correct flying star chart over your home – using compass directions as your markers – you can systematically study the quality and quantity of the luck of every sector and corner of your house. In this way, you can suppress any intangible bad energy and, likewise, enhance lucky good energy.

Flying star practice requires that you have a strong grounding in the fundamentals of feng shui; specifically, it requires an in-depth knowledge of the five elements – what they are, what they stand for, and their associated attributes (see page 9). In the ancient texts on flying star feng shui, the five-element theory is always cited as the basis for remedies and recommended enhancers.

Understand numbers to practice flying star   32

Note that the "stars" of flying star feng shui refer to numbers, and the flying star system is not unlike the study of numerology as applied to feng shui. Single numbers have good and bad connotations, lucky and unlucky meanings. Combinations of the numbers have deeper implications of good and bad luck, good fortune and misfortune. And, depending on the number of each of the wealth or the relationship "stars", they reveal the potential for wealth and relationship luck. Numbers, however, have different strengths, different potencies, and even different meanings during different periods of time. To practice flying star effectively to a high level, you have to become familiar with the meanings assigned to numbers, and also be aware of their relative strength at different time periods. We are currently in period 8, which began on February 4, 2004 and will last until 2024 – a period of 20 years. This is, therefore, an excellent time to add the dimension of "time" to your feng shui practice, since what is done in these early years of period 8 is likely to benefit you for the next two decades.

Meanings of numbers

The following meanings of flying star numbers are useful to bear in mind, as in order to identify the good and bad star numbers you need to know the meanings of the numbers from 1 to 9. Below is a simple summary, but for detailed information on each of the numbers and their meanings, see Tip 44.

* Numbers 2, 3, 5, and 7 bring afflictions. Use remedies to counter their effect on the space they occupy in your home.

* The numbers 1, 4, 6, and 8 bring bonanzas and great good fortune. The luckiest number of the four is 8. Collectively, numbers 1, 6, and 8 are known as the white numbers, for wherever they occur they bring good fortune. The number 4 brings love and education luck.

*Number 9 is a magnifying number, enhancing the effect of good and bad numbers wherever it occurs.

Only the numbers on your home's flying star chart count in flying star feng shui – not your house number.

All three numbers in each square of this flying star chart are analyzed to determine if they are auspicious or afflicted. However, the smaller numbers exert a greater influence and so are more important than the big numbers in the center.

5	9	9	5	5	6
	6		2		
6	8	4	1	2	
	5		7		
1	4	8	6	3	
	1		3		

33 20-year time frames are expressed as period 7 and period 8

In flying star feng shui we take note of the cycles of time, which the Chinese Hsia calendar uses to express the cyclical shifts of chi energy that affect the Universe. This calendar is slightly different from the traditional Chinese lunar calendar, and it uses February 4 as the start of the year. This is also the date that corresponds to the lap chun, what the Chinese refer to as the first day of spring.

Each cycle of time is divided into nine periods, with each period lasting 20 years. Every period exerts a particular influence on the energy distribution of the world, thereby affecting the feng shui of houses and buildings. Each period is ruled by a number from 1 to 9. So the whole cycle of time lasts 180 years, comprising nine periods of 20 years each.

Period 7 influences
The world has just completed the period of 7, which began on February 4, 1984 and ended on February 3, 2004. During the period of 7, the number 7 was the dominant lucky number, and it was a period when the West direction and the metal element dominated the feng shui slant of the world's consciousness. Money and wealth accumulation were, thus, particularly important during the period of 7. It also coincided with the rise in importance of women in high places and with money-making opportunities being concentrated in the western sectors of land-masses. It is not surprising that a great many new billionaires and multi-billion-dollar businesses mush-roomed (as personified by Bill Gates and the rise of online businesses generally) in the western part of the North American landmass all through the period of 7. But that period has now come to an end. So the number 7 has ceased to be an auspicious number and, instead, has become weak and negative.

Period 8 influences
We are now in the period of 8 and the chi energy of the world has been transformed into an earth period dominated by the trigram Ken, which represents the mountain, and is generally regarded as a period of introspection. Over the next 20 years, therefore, the focus will be more on health and relationships and, as we go deeper into the period, getting rich and making money will become less important than the softer issues of living, such as creating feelings of wellness and happiness, and confronting rela-tionship issues. This transformation will become increasingly evident in the coming few years.

In the Chinese lunar calendar, the New Year begins on February 4, or lap chun, the first day of spring.

Recognize flying star charts 34

Flying star charts apply to all buildings – houses, apartment blocks, offices, and other properties – that are built and completed, or massively renovated, within a 20-year period. Period 7 houses, for example, are those built or renovated between February 4, 1984 and February 4, 2004 – the 20 years ruled by the number 7. Hence, these buildings are referred to as period 7 buildings. Houses that are, or will be, built or renovated between February 4, 2004 and February 4, 2024 are known as period 8 houses. Houses deemed to belong to the current period are always said to have much more vigorous energy than those that belong to the immediately preceding period, and so have a greater potential to be lucky and auspicious.

The 24 directions

There are altogether 16 charts that show the distribution of luck in 16 types of home. The categorization of homes is based upon the facing direction of the building. There are in total 24 possible directions, and these refer to the three sub-directions of all eight directions of the compass. Thus, there will be South 1, South 2, and South 3, and North 1, North 2, and North 3 directions. So, every main direction of 45° marked in the compass is divided into three sub-directions that comprise 15° of the compass.

The essence of compass feng shui

For the purposes of categorizing houses and buildings, the flying star formula recognizes two facing directions per compass direction. Thus for houses facing South there are two charts – one for houses facing South 1 and another for houses facing South 2 and 3 (see the Lo Pan compass in Tip 30). It is the same for all eight major directions. So, for each period there are 16 different charts based on 16 types of house. In every house, the distribution of luck energy is different – in one type of house, certain corners are auspicious and other parts

Every building has a facing direction, determined by the compass, that forms the basis of its flying star chart.

are afflicted. Knowing this, the chi energy of the various rooms of the house can be enhanced or corrected, as the case may be. This is the essence of compass feng shui, so the first step to using flying star to improve the feng shui of your house calls for you to familiarize yourself with the charts and the numbers indicated.

Q & A

Q: *Why are there just two grids for three directions?*

A: Because the grids for the second and third sub-directions are always exactly the same. For example, there is one grid for South 1 and another for South 2 and South 3 because the grids for these second and third sub-directions are the same. So the grids are expressed as South 1 and South 2/3.

35   How to read a typical flying star chart

This is what a typical flying star chart looks like. It is made up of nine grids that mirror the nine squares of the Lo Shu square (the ancient formula found on the back of a tortoise in Chinese mythology). Inside each grid are three numbers. The large number is the Period star and shows the Period number in each sector. In the center grid, the Period number is 7, so we know this is a Period 7 chart. On the right of the Period star in every grid is a smaller number representing the water star, and on the left is a number representing the mountain star. This arrangement of numbers occurs in every grid.

How numbers reveal luck

All three numbers tell you something about the luck of the part of the house they correspond to. Remember that in flying star feng shui the compass is always used (see Tip 30). So, to know the luck of the Northwest corner of your home, you have to use the compass to identify the Northwest, and in the chart being used as an example here, that will be the

A flying star chart decoded

Three numbers appear in every square on a flying star chart. They reveal the luck of the sectors of your home.

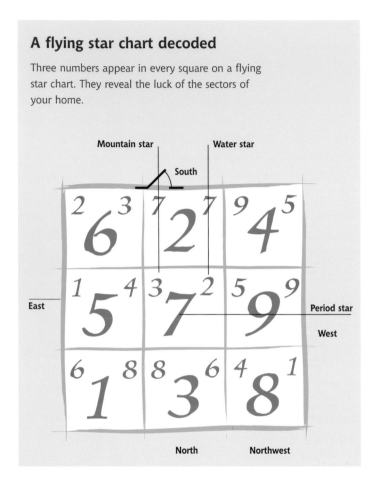

Mountain star · Water star · South · East · Period star · West · North · Northwest

corner where the Period star is 8 – a very lucky number. The water star is 1 and since 1 also represents water here, the water star is lucky. To activate its luck, place water (such as a pond, a pool, or an aquarium) here. The mountain star in the Northwest is 4, which stands for literary and scholastic success, and is also a lucky number. It can be activated with a crystal.

Activate the mountain star with natural quartz crystal.

Introducing water stars and mountain stars   36

Numbers indicate whether the water and mountain stars bring good luck or affliction. Water stars govern the luck of money, wealth, income, career, and material success. Mountain stars indicate relationship and health luck and generally specify whether or not a home has happy and joyous chi energy. In period 7, wealth accumulation governed the collective consciousness of the world and, thus, activating the auspicious water stars of the home tended to dominate. So making money and getting rich were the buzz words of period 7 because the ruling trigram, Tui, stands for the lake – water symbolizes money.

In period 8 it is the mountain stars that are far stronger, because in this period the ruling trigram, Ken, stands for mountain. Mountain stars suggest a time of preparation, when meditation, introspection, and a turning toward less materialistic pursuits become increasingly important. So, in period 8 you will find that there will be a heavier emphasis placed on relationships and the pursuit of inner wisdom.

Identifying the lucky water and mountain stars in your home shows you exactly which sectors to activate with water and which to energize with crystals in order to improve your feng shui. In fact, correctly energizing your auspicious water and mountain stars is such a powerful way to enjoy wealth and relationship luck that for this reason alone it is worth making the effort to accurately locate these auspicious stars.

The trigram Tui (top) stands for "lake". Ken (above) means "mountain."

37 Period 7 flying star charts

The flying star charts of Period 7 are reproduced here to enable you to analyze the distribution of luck in your house, apartment, or office, if it was built or extensively renovated anytime from February 4, 1984 to February 3, 2004. Even though we have now entered period 8, if your house was built or extensively renovated in period 7, the charts of this period will apply to your home. It is likely that most houses will be period 7 houses. Remember to choose the chart that corresponds to your home's facing direction.

Using a compass

Use a compass to identify the chart that applies to your house. Remember, the directions move in a clockwise direction. When your house is facing exactly South or North, for example, then you know that it faces the South 2 or North 2 direction. If your house is facing slightly to the left of South 2, then it is said to be facing South 1; if slightly to the right of South 2, it is facing South 3. Note that as we move strongly into period 8, all structures deemed to be period 7 will lose energy. At the same time, the number 7, which was lucky during period 7, has now turned ugly and violent. So note the period 7 charts that have the double 7 in the front or the back of the house, for it is these houses that will get into trouble during this period of 8, making it necessary to implement changes to transform the building into a period 8 one.

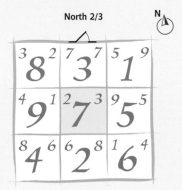

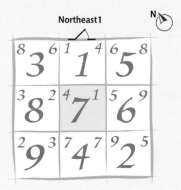

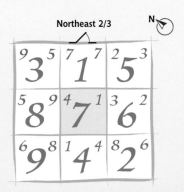

East 1
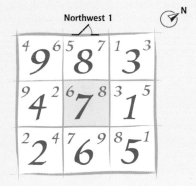

³1⁸	⁷5³	⁸6⁴
⁵3¹	⁹7⁵	⁴2⁹
¹8⁶	²9⁷	⁶4²

South 1

²6³	⁷2⁷	⁹4⁵
¹5⁴	³7²	⁵9⁹
⁶1⁸	⁸3⁶	⁴8¹

West 1

²4⁶	⁷9²	⁶8¹
⁹2⁴	⁵7⁹	¹3⁵
⁴6⁸	³5⁷	⁸1³

East 2/3

⁶1²	²5⁷	¹6⁶
⁴3⁹	⁹7⁵	⁵2¹
⁸8⁴	⁷9³	³4⁸

South 2/3

⁴6¹	⁸2⁶	⁶4⁸
⁵5⁹	³7²	¹9¹
⁹1⁵	⁷3⁷	²8³

West 2/3

⁸4³	³9⁷	⁴8⁸
¹2⁵	⁵7⁹	⁹3⁴
⁶6¹	⁷5²	²1⁶

Southeast 1

¹5⁸	⁹6⁷	⁴2²
⁵1³	⁸7⁶	²4⁹
³3¹	⁷8⁵	⁶9⁴

Southwest 1

⁵2⁹	⁷4⁷	³9²
⁹6⁵	¹7⁴	²8³
⁸5⁶	⁴1¹	⁶3⁸

Northwest 1

⁴9⁶	⁵8⁷	¹3³
⁹4²	⁶7⁸	³1⁵
²2⁴	⁷6⁹	⁸5¹

Southeast 2/3

⁶5⁴	⁷6⁵	³2¹
²1⁹	⁸⁺7⁶⁺	⁵4³
⁴3²	⁹8⁷	¹9⁸

Southwest 2/3

⁶2⁸	⁴4¹	⁸9⁶
²6³	¹7⁴	⁹8⁵
³5²	⁷1⁷	⁵3⁹

Northwest 2/3

⁸9¹	⁷8⁹	²3⁴
³4⁵	⁶7⁸	⁹1²
¹2³	⁵6⁷	⁴5⁶

38 Period 8 flying star charts

The flying star charts for period 8 houses are reproduced here (see right) to help those of you whose homes have only just been built or renovated (after February 4 2004). When houses are extensively renovated, it changes them into houses of the current period, and then you can use the current period's charts to give you an idea of the way the luck in your home is distributed. These period 8 charts are also useful for another reason – they enable you to make a comparison with period 7 houses to see which chart would serve you better, based on how the layout of your house fits into the respective luck maps.

Note that the lucky chi energy of homes built in period 8 tends to congregate around the middle of the vertical grids of the chart. This favors deep homes rather than shallow ones. As a rule of thumb, it is a good idea to have homes that are at least three rooms deep.

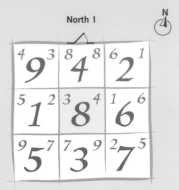

North 1

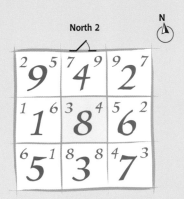

North 2

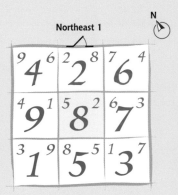

Northeast 1

Northeast 2/3

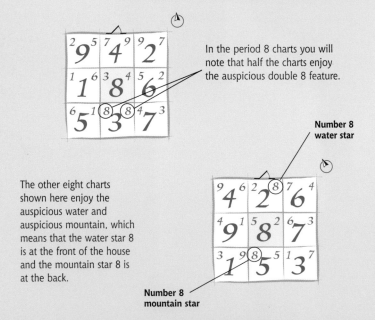

In the period 8 charts you will note that half the charts enjoy the auspicious double 8 feature.

The other eight charts shown here enjoy the auspicious water and auspicious mountain, which means that the water star 8 is at the front of the house and the mountain star 8 is at the back.

Number 8 water star

Number 8 mountain star

East1

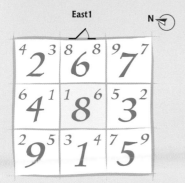 N

4 **2** 3	8 **6** 8	9 **7** 7
6 **4** 1	1 **8** 6	5 **3** 2
2 **9** 5	3 **1** 4	7 **5** 9

South 1

N

5 **7** 2	9 **3** 7	7 **5** 9
6 **6** 1	4 **8** 3	2 **1** 5
1 **2** 6	8 **4** 8	3 **9** 4

West 1

N

9 **5** 7	4 **1** 3	5 **9** 2
2 **3** 5	6 **8** 1	1 **4** 6
7 **7** 9	8 **6** 8	3 **2** 4

East 2

N

7 **2** 9	3 **6** 4	2 **7** 5
5 **4** 2	1 **8** 6	6 **3** 1
9 **9** 7	8 **1** 8	4 **5** 3

South 2

N

3 **7** 4	8 **3** 8	1 **5** 6
2 **6** 5	4 **8** 3	6 **1** 1
7 **2** 9	9 **4** 7	5 **9** 2

West 2/3

N

3 **5** 4	8 **1** 8	7 **9** 9
1 **3** 6	6 **8** 1	2 **4** 5
5 **7** 2	4 **6** 3	9 **2** 7

Southeast 1

N

7 **6** 5	8 **7** 6	4 **3** 2
3 **2** 1	9 **8** 7	6 **5** 4
5 **4** 3	1 **9** 8	2 **1** 9

Southwest 1

N

7 **3** 1	5 **5** 8	9 **1** 3
3 **7** 6	2 **8** 5	1 **9** 4
4 **6** 7	8 **2** 2	6 **4** 9

Northwest 1

N

9 **1** 2	8 **9** 1	3 **4** 5
4 **5** 6	7 **8** 9	1 **2** 3
2 **3** 4	6 **7** 8	5 **6** 7

Southeast 2/3

N

2 **6** 9	1 **7** 8	5 **3** 3
6 **2** 4	9 **8** 7	3 **5** 1
4 **4** 2	8 **9** 6	7 **1** 5

Southwest 2/3

N

6 **3** 9	8 **5** 2	4 **1** 7
1 **7** 4	2 **8** 5	3 **9** 6
9 **6** 3	5 **2** 8	7 **4** 1

Northwest 2/3

N

5 **1** 7	6 **9** 8	2 **4** 4
1 **5** 3	7 **8** 9	4 **2** 6
3 **3** 5	8 **7** 1	9 **6** 2

39 Identify the chart for your home

Each chart is based upon the facing direction of the house, so in order to identify the correct chart that applies to your home, first you will need to use a compass to determine its facing direction. Identifying the facing direction of a property can at times be challenging, since modular or irregular-shaped structures do not have a clear-cut facing direction. Besides, the facing direction of the main door is not always the same as the facing direction of the house itself. So you will need to make your judgment carefully (see Tip 40, opposite). The flying star chart also depends upon the age of your house – either when it was built, or when last extensively renovated.

Discovering your luck distribution

Before the recent surge in popularity of feng shui, flying star feng shui was out of reach of most people, and was accessible only to old-time feng shui practitioners. Here, I have made everything as easy as possible, so all you need do is correctly take the facing direction of your house and then see which one of the period 7 or 8 charts reproduced in this book applies to it (see Tips 37 and 38).

Next, use that chart to study the luck distribution of your home's layout. From there on, all you need do to make your home lucky is to apply the correct feng shui remedies to overcome the afflictions that cause misfortune, and enhance the chi that brings good fortune.

PROJECT

Three ways to update your home

To get the maximum benefit from your feng shui practice, you need to research the natal chart of your home based on the flying star method (see Tips 34 and 35). However, you must first transform your residence into a period 8 home. To do this, you need to change three types of energy in your home:

1 Change the Heaven energy by changing at least some part of your home's roof or, if you live in an apartment, some part of its ceiling.
2 Change the Earth energy by changing some part of your flooring.
3 Change your own Mankind energy by changing the main door.
Updating your home to a period 8 residence will be extremely beneficial because with the move into period 8 (which began on February 4, 2004) all houses can lose chi vitality unless these Heaven, Earth, and Mankind energies are revitalized. If you don't do this, you may discover that a great many afflictions start to build up in your residence – so it is best to update your property and enjoy the benefits of the new period of 8.

You can change your apartment to a period 8 building simply by painting your ceilings, which updates your Heaven energy.

Identify the facing direction of your home 40

To benefit from the compass formulas, it is necessary to determine the facing direction of the house correctly and accurately.

The facing direction of your home is not necessarily the same as the facing direction of your main front door. In most houses the main door and the house do face the same direction, but you should not assume that this is always the case. If they do face the same direction, then there is the potential for better feng shui. If they do not, then determining your facing direction requires some judgment on your part.

Making a decision

Take a good look at your house from all angles. Usually, its orientation is obvious to the eye and there are general guidelines to help you determine your home's facing direction. Having said this, there will be houses that present a challenge – modular or irregular houses, for example, are examples where some extra thought is likely to be required.

For most buildings, however, look for the direction where there is the promise of maximum energy – for example, where there is movement, activity, and people. Or, the facing direction can be where the house window faces a pleasant view, a "bright hall" (an attractive space in front of the main door, such as a path or courtyard), or a valley. Only when you have successfully identified your home's facing direction should you use the compass to take that direction.

Which way does your home face?

The direction your front door faces is not always the facing direction of your home. Check out the examples here before you decide.

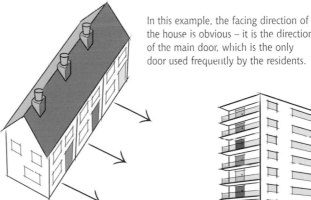

In this example, the facing direction of the house is obvious – it is the direction of the main door, which is the only door used frequently by the residents.

Here the official main door is blue, but the residents use the yellow side door most - which also faces the place of most yang energy, shown by the busy road nearby. So the facing direction of this home is the direction of the yellow door.

If you live in an apartment, the facing direction of your home is not necessarily that of your apartment's front door. You must take the facing direction of the door to your apartment block as your home's facing direction.

The facing direction of an apartment is always the facing direction of the block.

41   Are you certain of the facing direction?

When you are uncertain of your facing direction and you are reluctant to run the risk of using the wrong chart, it is a good idea to use two probable facing directions and the two corresponding charts. Then you can make a quick analysis of the luck of major rooms in the home to see which chart most accurately reflects your knowledge of the house's actual history. If you are lucky, there may be something very obviously revealed in one of the charts, such as a severe illness, some recent misfortune, or a bit of good luck, that makes one chart more likely than the other. Comparing two possible charts is one of the best ways to verify if your chart is the correct one for your house. Then, when you have decided which chart is most relevant to your experience of your home, it is possible to create excellent feng shui chi by enhancing the lucky areas. At the same time, you can also put remedies into place that overcome all the affliction stars bringing problems to the affected areas. If you have ever read books on flying star that tell you that using cures is futile, and that the only remedy is to vacate the affected rooms, I can categorically tell you that this is untrue. Every flying star feng shui affliction has a cure and that cure is almost always related to the theory of five elements or to the specialized amulet symbols for which China is so famous.

Symbolic feng shui

When you use formula feng shui it is vital to be familiar with symbolic feng shui – in other words, knowing the significance of symbols, shapes, colors, and the five elements. It is these things that are used as cures and enhancers based on what is revealed in the flying star charts. Knowledge of symbolic feng shui is what brings a superior level of effectiveness to your feng shui practice.

Symbolic feng shui means placing special feng shui symbols around the home for specific benefits. This is Sau, Chinese god of longevity.

When you have two possible facing directions

This home could have two facing directions – one for the back of the house, as shown, and another for the front. In this case, compare both flying star charts to see which is historically most accurate.

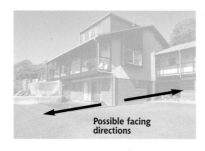

Possible facing directions

Read the flying star chart of your home   42

To apply the charts to your house, you need to superimpose them on a plan of your home's layout. This requires you to determine the compass sectors of the house. To do this:

- Use a good and reliable compass.

- Stand in the center of the house and identify all the different corners.

- Then transfer the three numbers of each compass sector to the corresponding sector of your house plan.

- This will immediately let you know the numbers that rule the luck of the different sectors of your house.

The numbers in each square tell you a great deal about the luck of the different sectors of your home; and it is the study of these numbers – what they each mean and how they relate to each other – that make up the

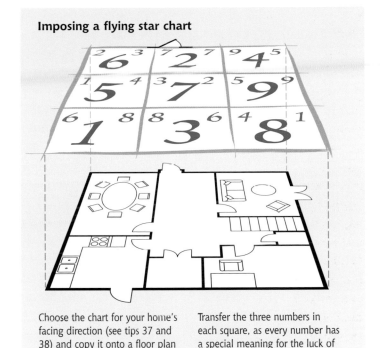

Imposing a flying star chart

Choose the chart for your home's facing direction (see tips 37 and 38) and copy it onto a floor plan of each level of your home.

Transfer the three numbers in each square, as every number has a special meaning for the luck of your home.

Q & A

Q: What do the three numbers in each square on a flying star chart mean?

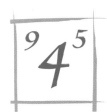

A: The large number in the center square is the period number, indicating the number that influences that square according to when the house was built or last underwent renovation. The little number on the right of the period number is the number of the water star. This indicates the wealth potential of the space indicated by that square. The little number on the left is the mountain star, indicating the relationship attributes and potential of the corner of the house represented by the square where that number occurs.

practice of flying star feng shui. In the old days, authentic feng shui masters would always use flying star methods to enhance the feng shui of spaces. This is because using this formula has the great advantage of being more exact and precise in pinpointing rooms that could be suffering from problems caused by time changes in chi energy.

So, the method addresses not just the spatial concepts of feng shui, but it also says a lot about the implications of time changes. Learning to read the flying star chart that applies to your house is the easiest and also the most effective way of practicing authentic Chinese feng shui.

43 Learning about annual and monthly charts

In addition to using the Period flying star chart of the house to feng shui your home, thereby ensuring it is not only a lucky house, but also a harmonious and peaceful one, it is also necessary to be aware of the annual and monthly flying star charts. These add the dimension of short-term updating to your home feng shui.

To do this requires you to follow the annual and monthly flying star charts. It is these charts that enable any practitioner systematically to update the feng shui of any house. Thus, every New Year it is incredibly beneficial to give your home a "sweep" of where the auspicious areas are located in that year, and also to where the afflictions of the year have flown.

Take note that all the different afflictions of misfortunes, accidents, loss, ill health, quarrels, and so on are represented by the different numbers from 1 to 9, and it is by sorting through the numbers that fly to different corners of the house that a full and accurate analysis can be made. Only then can you update your cures and enhancers each year.

What are annual and monthly charts?

The annual and monthly charts look just like the Period 7 or Period 8 charts, each with nine squares on a grid.

Shown here is the annual chart for 2006. You will see in this chart that the number in the middle is 3, which is referred to as the "Lo Shu number" of the year. In 2007, the number of the year will be 2, So, in annual charts the center number follows a backward sequence. Only nine numbers are used, so after the number 9 appears in the middle, the year after that will be 1 again.

In addition, the annual chart also shows the place of the three killings as well as the place where the god of the year, known as the Grand Duke Jupiter, resides. To access the charts for 2007 and beyond, visit the extensive online feng shui resource center at www.wofs.com and you will see not only the annual chart updated, but also the monthly charts.

As shown in this 2006 chart, the Grand Duke is in the Northwest while the place of the three killings is in the North.

	SE	S	SW
	2 Illness	7 Burglary	9 Lucky
E	1 Lucky	3 2006 Fire dog	5 5 Yellow	W
	6 Lucky	Auspicious 8 3 Killings	Gr Duke 4 ♥ Peach ♥ blossom
	NE	N	NW

De-code flying star numbers 44

In Flying Star feng shui, numbers 1 to 9, which appear on every flying star chart, all have particular meaning, singly or in combination. Here is a summary of their influence on your home:

- **Numbers 2 and 5:** Beware, as these two numbers stand for sickness and misfortune. Whenever they appear in any flying star chart, whether it is the chart of your house or the annual or month charts, take note that if you sleep, work, or eat in the sectors they appear in, you will suffer ill-health and misfortune.

- **Number 3** is the number of aggravation, quarrels, and hostility. This is the number that brings problems and misunderstandings. It also causes residents afflicted by it to have to cope with legal problems and unpleasant encounters with authorities. It must be kept under control, otherwise it will make your life hell if you become its victim.

- **Number 4** is excellent for scholarship and literary ambitions. It is also considered to be the number for romance, bringing love and even marriage when properly activated.

The number 4 on a flying star chart represents learning and literary ambitions.

- **Number 9** is a magnifying number, making the bad numbers worse and the good numbers better. It is also regarded as the number indicating future prosperity.

- **Number 7** was very auspicious in the last Period, but period 7 ended on February 4 2004. Now this same number is associated with violence and burglary. Those whose homes enjoyed the double 7 in the last 20 years will discover that, now we are in period 8, it has become dangerous and must be countered (see Tip 123).

- **Numbers 1, 6, and 8** are considered to be the "white" numbers and are excellent bringers of luck. Of the three, 8 reigns supreme, as this is period 8. The number 1 is lucky, but 6 is weak and does not have much strength unless aided by assistant numbers, such as 1 and 8. Together, this combination of numbers is believed to be hugely auspicious.

The numbers 1, 6, and 8 together are very auspicious – and identify a home's special luck sector. Here, for a North 1-facing home, the 1, 6, and 8 fall in the Northeast.

The water star is 8,

the mountain star is 6

the period star is 1

1 8	4 3	6 1
9 9	5 7	3 5
5 4	9 2	7 6

45 Locate the illness star 2 in your home

In flying star the number 2 is to be feared if you are old or suffering from a severe ailment, chronic or acute. When it appears as the water star 2, it suggests that your wealth luck is sick and your life is in need of some slowing down. If the mountain star is 2, it suggests double trouble, since it means that both the health and the relationships of residents living in that corner of your home, as well as in the whole building, will suffer.

Protecting your wellbeing

When the illness star 2 appears as a mountain or water star, note that its impact is magnified, so you will need to take its consequences very seriously. If good health is of concern to you, identify the flying star chart (be it period 7 or 8) that applies to your house and then circle the number 2 where it appears. This will immediately pinpoint the corners and sectors of your home suffering from this affliction.

In order to locate the afflicted sectors of your home, you will need to use a proper feng shui compass (see Tip 31). Consulting a floor plan of your home is extremely helpful for this exercise, since it is easier to find directions on a paper plan than by wandering from room to room with a compass. Once you have identified the place of the illness star, all you need do is suppress it with the correct symbols and elements (see Tip 46).

The illness star 2 affects the energy of your home just as do an external feng shui afflictions, but the illness star's location is time-sensitive, moving around different sectors of the home over the course of a month, year, and 20-year period. The illness star 2 can disrupt the wellbeing of you and others who share your home.

Locating the illness star 2

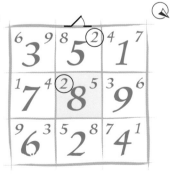

Illness star 2 is a mountain star when it appears on the right and a water star when it appears on the left of the central, or period, number.

Q & A

Q: *What if my house or apartment number includes the "bad" number 2?*

A: This does not matter, because numbers are not analysed in the same way as the flying star method. So although 2 indicates negative outcomes in a flying star analysis, it does not indicate bad luck when it occurs as part of an address number for homes or office buildings. To know if your house number is lucky or unlucky, you need to use numerology methods.

Ensure good health and longevity   46

Under the system of the five elements (see page 8), the illness star is believed to belong to the earth element and, as such, metal energy, especially yang metal energy, would be a great remedy.

The wu lou

One of the best symbols of good fortune is the brass wu lou. I use brass because the metal is strong and heavy. The wu lou is an amazingly powerful symbol of good health and long life. It is the symbol carried by the god of longevity, by the Goddess Kuan Yin, and by one of the Taoist Eight Immortals. It is said to be the container for the nectar of immortality. Thus, having the wu lou nearby is an excellent energizer for good health. But the wu lou, when it is made of brass, is also a powerful antidote against the illness star, since its metallic energy will suppress whatever illness chi is in the air.

The wu lou is a powerful feng shui symbol used to counteract bad illness chi.

The Buddhist Madonna, Kuan Yin, is often shown carrying the wu lou, a feng shui emblem of good health and a long life.

This benevolent goddess is loved by many Chinese people as a symbol of physical and emotional healing who bestows compassion and unconditional love.

Windchimes

Another excellent cure is the all-metal (brass) six-rod windchime – the sound of the metal provides the all-powerful cure. Six rods stand for big metal, and each time the wind blows the chimes it is creating yang metal chi. Do note, however, that the chimes are ineffective as a cure unless they are made completely of metal.

If your bedroom is afflicted by the illness star of the year or of your house flying star chart, you must use the windchime cure.

47   Stay clear of the quarrelsome star 3

There is another affliction that can potentially be even more damaging than the illness star 2 – this is the number 3 hostility star, also known as the bull-fighting quarrelsome star affliction. When your bedroom or main front door is afflicted by the presence of the number 3, you will have problems related to misunderstandings, quarrels, anger, and hostility that can easily escalate. Number 3 is a Wood star, so when it occurs in the East or Southeast its effect becomes even more dangerous and fierce.

Water or mountain star

When the number 3 occurs as the water star, it suggests quarrels relating to financial affairs, and if it occurs as the mountain star it brings anger and quarrels into otherwise healthy, happy relationships. More divorces and separations are caused by the number 3 star than people realize, and I have often said that divorces are often caused by feng shui afflictions such as this. The number 3 star also appears in the annual as well as the monthly charts, and when they all occur together in the same grid, and if that grid happens to correspond to your bedroom, you will definitely be well advised to move out.

If the star number 3 falls in the sector of your bedroom, relationship problems can result.

48   Deal with the number 3 star

The best remedy for the number three star is fire energy, which means the color red and the triangular shape. So the most effective cure is a three-dimensional triangular red crystal. This is a very powerful antidote to the number 3 star, and my advice has always been that if you do not know flying star feng shui you can place such a symbol on your office desk to ensure that, all through the year, you never succumb to the horrible effects of the number 3 star. Absolutely no harm will come from keeping this symbol near you. The fire energy in something such as a small crystal will bring only positive energy. Placed on a brass or gold-colored base, the triangular crystal will become an even more powerful antidote against the number 3 star.

Other techniques

Alternative cures for the hostile 3 star include red curtains, red cushion covers, or a red painting hung on one of the walls of the afflicted room. Bear in mind that the reason for using red is the need for its fire energy to exhaust the hostile wood star. You can also use red glitter lamps to simulate yang fire chi.

Locate the deadly 5 yellow star in your house chart   49

In flying star feng shui, the most dangerous affliction is known as the 5 yellow. This is the number 5 star, and it brings a variety of misfortunes to wreak havoc on the peace and tranquility of any house, especially when the 5 yellow afflicts the sector where the main door is located. The 5 yellow is most powerful when in the South, as the fire energy here gives it added strength. Once you have identified the flying star chart that applies to your house – again based on its facing direction and also on whether it is a period 7 or period 8 house – look for where the number 5 appears.

The feng shui enemy

When the number 5 is the large period number in the chart, it does bring misfortune, although its effects are nowhere near as powerful as when the 5 occurs as a water or mountain star number – the smaller numbers to the right and left, respectively, of the period number.

If the number 5 on your flying star chart falls in the location of your bedroom, you will need to use symbolic feng shui cures – see Tip 50. The best cure for the 5 yellow is metal energy, which includes the sound of metal – so metal windchimes are ideal.

When the 5 yellow is the water star, it causes financial loss to residents living in the sector where it occurs, and when it is the mountain star it causes relationships to break apart and also the loss of loved ones. The 5 yellow is, therefore, the feng shui enemy of any house and should be kept firmly under control. It is also very powerful when it occurs in earth corners such as the Northwest, the Southwest, and the center.

Annual and monthly confluence

The 5 yellow also makes its appearance in the annual feng shui chart, as well as in the monthly charts, and when they occur together in the same compass sector, that sector is said to be strongly afflicted. If your main door or bedroom happens to be located in the part of the house where it occurs, it is likely residents will suffer some form of misfortune, loss, or accident unless the 5 yellow has been suppressed. Merely moving out of the afflicted part of the house is not really a solution, since bad energy has a way of leaking into other sectors. It is vital, therefore, to place cures against the 5 yellow.

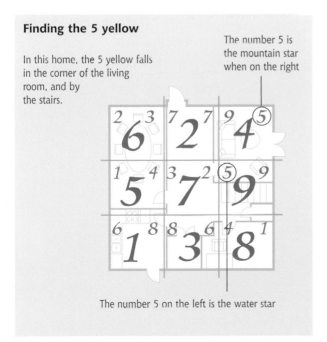

Finding the 5 yellow

In this home, the 5 yellow falls in the corner of the living room, and by the stairs.

The number 5 is the mountain star when on the right

The number 5 on the left is the water star

50 Overcome the 5 yellow star and keep it under control

Because the 5 yellow is regarded as an earth star, the best way to remedy its effects is to use metal chi energy to exhaust its strength. This is why metal windchimes were traditionally the cures recommended by the ancient feng shui masters.

The best windchimes are those with six hollow rods of equal size hanging from a round, metallic base to signify Heaven energy. This type of windchime captures bad chi and transforms it into good chi. The windchimes should be made completely of metal, and it is really best to use brass. Better yet are windchimes that have a center coin, also made of metal, depicting the astrological signs of the Chinese zodiac. The sound of metal on metal makes this type of windchime a much more powerful cure.

Hanging decorative chimes can help energize and enhance your space, but to neutralize the effects of the 5 yellow you will need to use a six-rod windchime, ideally made from brass (see below).

PROJECT
Extra measures

In the current period 8, which ends in 2024, an even more powerful cure for the 5 yellow is required because this is an earth period, which makes the 5 yellow very strong. Although the metal windchime is still an excellent cure, it may not be sufficient. So in period 8 the best cure for suppressing the 5 yellow is the five-element pagoda. Placing this pagoda in the 5 yellow sector will very effectively exhaust its energy.

Hang windchime here from a bracket or the ceiling

Place pagoda here

Diagnose and remedy flying star afflictions 51

Unless the flying star afflictions of your home are properly diagnosed and remedied it is difficult for you to enjoy good feng shui. This method of feng shui was once thought of as being extremely difficult and beyond the ability of lay people with no knowledge of or tradition in feng shui. Today, however, I have shown that it is not really that tough to learn flying star. The secret is to do away with all the Chinese code words that make it so hard for non-Chinese-speaking people to learn. Even Chinese-educated people found the old texts on flying star feng shui (known collectively as Zuan Kong feng shui) completely unintelligible. This was due to the code words used to denote the different compass directions. In this book I have used simple English to convey the essence of feng shui recommendations, making it as easy as possible for almost anyone to use this powerful formula to create a warm and happy home for themselves year after year.

Find out how old your house is, and when it was last renovated, to discover if your home is period 7 or period 8.

Dealing with the afflictions

Here is what you need to do to take care of the intangible afflictions affecting your house:

1 Use a compass to find your home's facing direction.

2 Determine the period in which your house was built or last renovated.

3 Determine which of the flying star charts (period 7 or 8 – see Tips 37 and 38) applies to your house.

4 Look out for the negative numbers that bring afflictions to the household (see Tip 32).

5 Systematically display remedies to keep all the afflictions at bay.

These glass wish-fulfilling "jewels" can be used to strengthen good mountain stars – numbers 1, 6, or 8. For bad numbers such as 2 or 5, use metal energy to exhaust them and protect health and relationship luck.

52

Take advantage of the auspicious numbers 1, 6, and 8

You should not get the impression that flying star charts have only negative numbers that bring afflictions. There are also positive numbers that bring good fortune, and foremost among these are what are often referred to as the "white numbers". These are the numbers 1, 6, and 8. These three numbers are said to bring excellent luck to residents of sectors corresponding to them.

The numbers 1, 6, and 8 are seen as particularly lucky in feng shui. You can incorporate these numbers in subtle ways in your home furnishings, as shown in this wall hanging.

Look out for the number 8 when it is used decoratively, in patterns or even knots.

The power of eight

Of the three white numbers, the most powerful good-fortune number is 8. This is because while it is already a lucky number (this being the Period of 8), it brings what the Taoists describe as the concept of double goodness,

a double good-fortune effect. So when the number appears in the sector where the front door is located or even where there is any door, it brings in the good-fortune chi energy. For example, in the year 2005, the number 8 was located in the South, so if your door is located in the South sector of your house you will have enjoyed great good fortune that year.

The number 6 is also a lucky number, signifying luck from heaven. But as this is period 8, the number 6 does not have much strength and it is not as strong as 8. The number 1, meanwhile, is also lucky, and in this period it stands for prosperity and good fortune in the distant future. The number 1 also stands for success, especially career success, and it brings good luck to your work. If the number 1 star occurs as the mountain star it signifies success in all your relationships; if it occurs as the water star, it means success in money-making matters.

The number 9 is the magnifying star 53

The number 9 is usually regarded as the magnifying star. Alone, 9 is a very auspicious number, symbolizing completion as well as the fullness of heaven and earth. In period 8 it is also regarded as the star of future prosperity. This is because it is the number immediately following the current period number, so it stands for the prosperity that will come after the current period of 8 is over, in about 20 years from now. In addition, we all want our prosperity and good fortune to last beyond this period, so the 9 is in this sense as important as the 8.

The number 9 magnifies the good or bad effects of any other number it falls beside on a flying star chart.

Good and bad

However, the 9 is also regarded as a magnifying number, so when it combines with good numbers (such as 1, 6, and 8) it enhances their good effects. When it combines with negative numbers, however (such as 2, 3, and 5), it likewise enhances their pernicious effects. So, whenever you see the 9 combined with the numbers 2, 3, or 5 in any flying star chart or annual and monthly charts, you know that it signals increased danger.

The number 4 is the romance star 54

The star number that stands for romantic luck is the 4, and it is best and strongest in its good effects when it comes as the mountain star. Then, all your love

On an annual flying star chart, look out for the number 4 if you want to improve your existing relationships or find new romance.

relationships will bring you happiness and come to a fruitful and happy conclusion. Love relationships refer to the type that leads to marriage. When the romance star 4 occurs, however, all married couples must strive to ensure that there should not be any type of water feature placed in the sector of the home corresponding to that number. The presence of water will lead to unhappiness and scandals of a sexual nature. And then it is a case of romantic infidelities being discovered, usually leading to unhappiness and the break-up of otherwise good relationships.

The number 4 in an annual chart indicates peach blossom luck, which brings romantic liaisons and marriage opportunities. In the year 2005, for example, the number 4 is in the center of the annual chart, and so this means that 2005 is a year when the incidence of people falling love will increase.

55 Activate the auspicious mountain and water stars in your chart

There have been quite a few references to mountain and water stars. Remember that these are the small numbers flanking the large number in any flying star chart. The mountain star represents the health and relationship luck of the sector, while the water star represents prosperity luck.

Natural crystal can be used to energize mountain energy, whereas the presence of water stimulates the wealth luck associated with water.

Mountain stars

When the mountain star is a lucky number, such as 8, it brings good-fortune relationship luck. It also brings excellent health luck, as the mountain star also stands for health. When the mountain star is lucky, it should be activated for the good fortune to manifest, but when it is unlucky it should be suppressed or exhausted. The mountain star's good-luck effect usually only manifests itself when the presence of a mountain symbol energizes it. This can be a real mountain or hill in the direction of the sector it occupies, or it can be a painting. The energizing symbol can also be a large, natural crystal or geode.

Water stars

The water star stands for wealth luck and, like the mountain star, when its numbers are lucky, such as when the 8 occurs, then its good effects should be activated by the presence of water. Indeed, this is one of the best ways to feng shui for wealth. When the water star 8 is activated by the presence of water, residents are almost certain to become rich, or at least see their incomes significantly improved. Nothing makes for a happier home than for its residents to grow richer. Water stars 6 and 1 are also very auspicious.

Employ flying star enhancers and remedies 56

While the method of the flying star is technical, requiring charts to be drawn up and taking account of time periods, its effective practice requires the use of symbolic remedies. Hence, a good knowledge of symbolic feng shui is also required before you can effectively use the enhancers and remedies that magnify good fortune and suppress misfortune. All the authentic masters of the old days who use flying star methods are also very knowledgeable when it comes to the symbolic meanings and properties of objects and decorative images.

The use of symbols

Since feng shui is a Chinese practice, I usually recommend Chinese cultural symbols of good fortune as enhancers. Likewise, I also turn to Chinese symbols of protection for the remedies. However, it is important to stress that symbols from other cultures when they are used correctly are also equally effective. It is important only that you understand the basis

PROJECT

Windchimes and more

When you need to overcome the illness-bringing star number 2, it is a good idea to use yang metal energy. As alternatives or additions to using windchimes, look for objects that are made of any type of metal – such as brass, copper, gold, silver, or steel – and which also have movement. A good example would be table or floor-standing fans made of metal. To overcome the effects of the very harmful star number 5, the metal energy required can be yin or yang metal. In this case, a large brass table or brass container would be excellent, along with containers and decorative objects made of metal. You can also use symbols of good fortune made

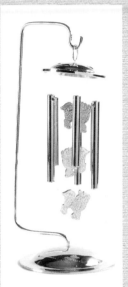

from metal, crystal, wood, or glass – for example, the fish hook is a symbol of auspicious good fortune in New Zealand based on their traditional Maori culture, so placing such as symbol in the home would signify good fortune enhancement.

You can use polished crystals to symbolize the power of the five Chinese elements – red for Fire, green for Wood, white for Metal, yellow for Earth, and blue for Water.

of using specific symbols or cures. This usually means understanding the yin and yang of symbols as well as their elemental nature. This is because so much of feng shui is based on the three cycles of the five elements. Thus, enhancing symbols use the productive cycle of the elements, while remedies usually use the exhaustive cycles. So, in order to overcome the illness star 2 and the 5 yellow, you need yang metal energy – you can find a substitute for the windchime and five-element pagoda if you so wish from your own culture.

57 Locating auspicious stars and afflictions when your home is an irregular shape

When you have determined the facing direction of your home (see Tips 19, 40, and 41) and looked up the flying star chart that relates to your home's facing direction (see Tips 37 and 38), the shape of your home may cause confusion when you come to copy the chart's numbers onto a floor plan. If your property is a perfect square, then it's easy to impose the square chart – but most homes are an irregular shape. If your home is semi-detached, or you have had a room extended or your house remodeled in some way, it's likely you will have missing sectors, or areas of the chart that fall outside the boundaries of your home. This means that you may miss out on some auspicious luck sectors – symbolized by the numbers 1, 4, 6, 8, and 9 (see Tip 32) but equally, you can benefit because you will be less afflicted by the misfortune stars 2, 3, 5, and 7, because a smaller proportion of space is "hit" by these numbers.

Ground floor of property with adjoining wall

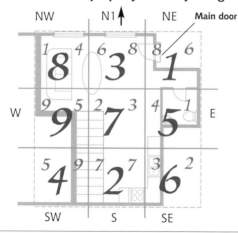

This home faces North 1 and is period 7 (see Tips 30 and 37). Note that the facing direction of the house is not the direction of the main door, but the two large windows at the front of the house – this is the place of the most yang energy, and hence the facing direction. The lucky sectors are the foyer and the sitting room.

Ground floor of two-floor apartment or maisonette

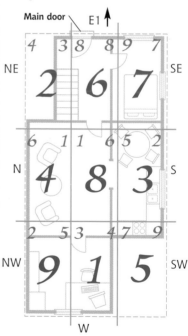

This home faces East 1 and is period 8 (see Tips 30 and 38). The lucky sectors are the hall, in the center grid, which features the very auspicious numbers 1, 6, and 8, and note the special double-8 in the foyer, which brings excellent luck to all the home's inhabitants.

Ground floor of detached house with extension to kitchen

This home faces South 1 and is period 8. Note that the chart is not laid over the garage area, because this is not a designated living space. However, if on the second floor a bedroom or other room has been built over the garage, this would be included when laying the chart over a plan of the whole upper floor. Here, note the auspicious double-8 feature that falls in the location of the kitchen.

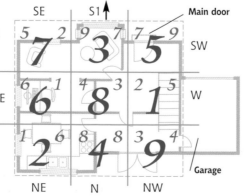

Bad energy can be invisible and intangible 58

A principal cornerstone of practicing feng shui is always to be alert to the afflictions that cause misfortune. It is all very well using feng shui to try to get rich or gain success, but what is more important to many people is making sure that their everyday lives are not shaken by serious accidents or tragic events. And it is feng shui's ability to help us be aware of afflictions before they happen that makes it such an invaluable living skill to acquire.

Feng shui acknowledges that bad energy, which causes bad things to happen, can and often is invisible and also intangible. This intangible energy is not necessarily caused by the physical structures in our living environment, but rather by the passage of time. Effective feng shui practice takes the fullest account of the intangible effects of chi, because only then is it possible to identify when and where misfortune can strike. Prevention is then possible either by moving yourself out of the afflicted spaces or, better yet, by installing remedies that reduce the effect of the bad chi energy. It is, therefore, extremely useful to acquaint yourself with the time dimension of feng shui.

Changing periods in a 180-year cycle 59

In time-dimension feng shui, time is divided into periods, and a full cycle of a time period lasts for 180 years. These 180 years are divided into nine periods that last 20 years each, and every period is "ruled," or dominated, by a number from 1 to 9. According to the texts that deal with time-dimension feng shui, each of the 20-year periods manifests the attributes of the number that dominates that period. So every period will have its characteristic strength and weakness, will favor the rise of men or women, and will bring different kinds of chi energy to homes.

Adding an extra dimension

Every time the period changes, the map of chi energy within all the built-up structures of the world will also change according to how it is influenced by the new period. The most immediate effect is that while the number that dominates the current period is strong and usually brings extreme good fortune, once its reign ends it will transform into a weak number. It loses energy and if it is a number that originally brings misfortunes, it will revert to its original nature. Thus, the numbers 5,

A feng shui "period" lasts for 20 years, and changes over on February 4.

The periods date from 1–9 in a 180-year cycle. In the current period 8, the positive numbers are 1, 4, 6, 8, and 9.

2, and 3 can be regarded as bad numbers that bring misfortunes; but they can also bring auspicious good fortune in periods that are ruled by them. So knowing about time periods in feng shui enables you to add an extra dimension to your feng shui practice.

60   Implications of period 7 coming to a end

The end of period 7 means that most houses in the world immediately lose energy. This is because it is likely that most of them would have been either built or renovated in the 20 years between February 4 1984 and February 4 2004, thereby making them period 7 houses. According to feng shui principles, however, as soon as the period changes, the energy of the preceding period's number loses vitality and strength. This means that period 7 houses need to be revitalized and re-energized as soon as possible so that we can welcome in the chi energy of the new period 8.

A change of luck

A second major implication is that the number 7, which was such a lucky number all through period 7, has now reverted to its original true nature, which is bad. The number 7 star brings burglary luck as well as violence and bloodshed. Not for no reason is it called the red star 7, and its element is metal. For 20 years this aspect of its nature was overshadowed by its good side. For 20 years the number 7 brought a great deal of luck to the many people living in period 7 houses. But the same people who benefited from the number 7 are now poised to suffer its bad side, unless they re-energize their house and transform it into a period 8 home.

61   The current period 8 and its influences

Inner values become more pertinent than external wealth and materialism as we feel the influence of the new period 8, which began on February 4, 2005.

With the change in period, the number 8 now becomes very lucky indeed. The number 8 is already a very lucky number by itself, and during the previous 20 years it signified "future prosperity." In its own period, the number 8 represents current prosperity, while the number 9 signifies future prosperity.

Changing fortunes

During the current period we will see attitudes transforming – for example, while 7 was a period that favored women, the number 8 favors young men, and its ruling trigram is the mountain, which stands for a time of preparation, or getting ready. The mountain also governs health luck and the luck of relationships. It is a time when the pursuit of knowledge is more important than the pursuit of wealth. In the coming 20 years there will be a refocusing toward family values and moral behavior.

Making money will become less important than the quality of lifestyle and having time to enjoy the family. Period 8 favors everyone whose Kua number is 8 (see Tip 89), and such people will find themselves very lucky indeed. And those living on the Northeast and Southwest axis – meaning those living in houses that face either the Southwest or the Northeast – will benefit hugely from the energies of the new period.

Checking your house period and its implications   62

Because the impact of these period changes is actually very serious, and the time dimension exerts such a strong influence on everyone's feng shui, if you wish to tap into the good luck of the current period 8 you should definitely consider some major renovation-type changes to your home to bring it in line with the chi energy of the new period. In any event, you should check the flying star chart of your house if it belongs to period 7 (see Tip 37), and determine the problem areas that have now arisen in your feng shui due to the period changeover. Many readers will discover they are now living in a period 7 house, and an analysis of the building's flying star chart should further reveal the negative implications of failing to change its period.

Assess your past good fortune

The main drawback of not changing the period energy of your home lies in the negative energy now brought by the number 7 star. In the past 20 years, the number 7 brought exceedingly good fortune, especially to houses facing South, Southwest, North, and Northeast.

These houses benefited from the double 7s in the front or back of their houses. It brought luck and good relationships in period 7, but now in the new period the number 7 brings burglary, violence, and bloodshed. Unless you control the 7 star with water it will bring a great deal of misfortune to your home. This alone is good enough reason to transform your home's chi energy – see Tips 63 and 64 overleaf.

With the advent of period 8, the energy of your home has changed, which brings new challenges and success potential.

63 Changing your home into a period 8 home

If you decide to change the energy of your house or apartment into period 8 energy, some planning is required. There is bound to be digging, banging, and knocking involved, so the first thing you need to do is turn to the section on annual afflictions (see Tips 115–129) and note which corners are the auspicious sectors of your home (where renovation should begin and end) and which are the afflicted sectors that, ideally, should be left alone.

Take great care

When undertaking renovation work that involves digging, banging, and disturbing the energy, it is crucial to avoid disturbing the places of the Grand Duke Jupiter, the three killings, and the deadly 5 yellow (see Tips 118, 120, and 121) – these are the three places you really must not renovate, otherwise bad luck in the form of illnesses, accidents, and misfortunes is sure to materialize. Thus, changing your home to period 8 is not a simple exercise, but it is one worth undertaking if you wish to attract seriously good feng shui luck that will last for the next 20 years

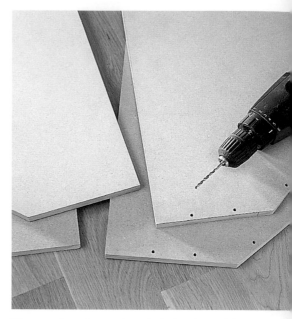

When carrying out renovations, don't do noisy work in unlucky sectors – this disturbs energy and is thought to result in misfortune in the home.

until February 4, 2024.

Remember how to update

Here's a reminder of how to change the period of your home from 7 to 8:

- Change the building's heaven energy by changing the roof tiles.

- Change the building's earth energy by changing the floor, garden decking, or turf.

- Change the building's humankind energy by changing its main door.

In general, at least one-third of the roof, floor, or garden area will need to be retiled, replaced, or returfed. You can buy a new front door, but if you are on a budget, consider giving the old door a fresh coat of paint.

For people living in apartments, repaint your ceiling to change the heaven chi (see Tip 39).

Q & A

Q: What if I can't avoid renovating in unlucky sectors?

A: If you must renovate or carry out essential maintenance work, as long as you do not start or end your renovations in any sector that is afflicted, you should be fine. As long as you plan your renovations taking note of all the afflictions of the year, you will avoid activating misfortune stars and suffering their effects in your life.

A shortcut way to welcome period 8   64

If it is truly impossible to change your house energy to that of period 8, then the next best way to welcome in the new earth chi is to create an opening in the Northwest sector of your house. An opening here would mean a door, a sliding opening, or a large window. It should be as large as possible to welcome in the new chi.

Why the northwest?

This is because in period 7 the number 8 was in the Northwest sector, so the period 8 energy comes from the Northwest. Making an opening in this sector thus welcomes in the period 8 energy. In fact, in all houses it is always a good idea to have some type of opening in the Northwest, since this is the place that signifies the Patriarch. Having an opening here implies that fresh, new energy is always available to replenish whatever is lost. This benefits the family breadwinner.

A door or window in the Northwest is a sure way to bring in the new energy of period 8. If you already have a small window in this sector, you could enlarge it, or at least clean glass doors or windows in the sector, wash and re-hang curtains or blinds, and hang new drapes to symbolically welcome new chi.

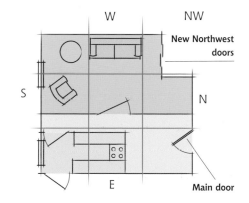

Opening up the Northwest
In this property, the Northwest sector has been opened up by adding sliding doors, which give access to a sheltered garden area.

Part Two

Creating a Powerfully Auspicious and Happy Home

CAPTURING THE INFLUENCE OF MOUNTAIN AND WATER STARS

If you want to live a happy life in which aggravations are kept to a minimum, make every effort to activate the mountain star energy within your home, and particularly now that we are in the period of the mountain star – period 8 coincides with the trigram Ken, which stands for the mountain. It is thus an earth period, and mountain star energy reigns supreme. This is the chi energy that rules the quality of all the relationships in our lives.

Mountain stars also signify our state of health. When the mountain star number indicated is an auspicious number such as 8, then it indicates that health luck is strong. If the mountain star is unlucky, such as 2, 3, or 5, it indicates danger regarding health matters. In this situation, mountain stars need to be exhausted with symbolic and element cures.

In the same way that auspicious-numbered mountain stars bring good relationship luck, water stars that are represented by lucky numbers bring wealth luck. When properly activated and energized, auspicious water stars attract higher incomes and excellent short- and long-term money luck.

Auspicious mountain stars enhance relationship luck 65

For relationships to be positive, they need to be activated by the presence of crystal energy or fire energy, which in the element cycle produces earth (see page 9). Crystals are the vast treasures of the earth, found deep under the ground and inside mountains. Crystals are the ultimate earth energy energizer, because contained within any rock crystal are millions of years of concentrated earth energy. That is why crystals will be such good and excellent feng shui over the next 20 years.

Loving relationships

Use natural crystals to energize the auspicious mountain stars of homes and buildings. When placed inside homes in the sectors where the mountain star numbers are auspicious, such as 8, 6, 1, or 4, it will attract and create happy relationships. These relationships could be between man and wife, siblings, colleagues, or friends, as well as between fathers and sons,

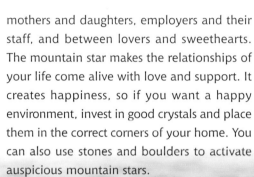

The numbers 1, 6, and 8 attract happy relationships.

mothers and daughters, employers and their staff, and between lovers and sweethearts. The mountain star makes the relationships of your life come alive with love and support. It creates happiness, so if you want a happy environment, invest in good crystals and place them in the correct corners of your home. You can also use stones and boulders to activate auspicious mountain stars.

66   Mountain stars exert influence over health and longevity

Activating the auspicious mountain star corners of your home will simultaneously help you enjoy longevity and the luck of good health. This is because the mountain star also governs the health luck of residents. Another course of action is to ensure that the sectors where auspicious mountain stars reside are not harmed or killed off by the presence of too many tall trees or of large amounts of metal.

Too much wood or too many trees can symbolically destroy the energy of a home's earth sector, which may deplete the residents' good health. In the cycle of elements (see page 9) wood destroys earth, or mountain, energy.

Based on the five-element theory, please always remember that wood energy destroys earth energy and that metal energy exhausts earth energy. Keeping your car parked in a corner where a lucky mountain star resides, for example, would mean that the amount of heavy metal in that sector destroys the good luck brought by the mountain star.

67   Use a geode to simulate the physical presence of mountains

Another way to activate and energize the auspicious mountain star corner is to bring into your home a large geode of crystal. This can create a very powerful reaction indeed, and residents who are sensitive to earth energy may discover that it is, in fact, too powerful. If so, then use a smaller piece of geode.

A crystal geode is a natural crystal formation inside a rock, which you can place in your home to activate mountain energy.

Salt lamps

Do not under any circumstances display what are referred to as "salt lamps". These look like crystals of the pink and yellow variety and, indeed, they are chunks of salt, which is of course a crystalline substance. Inside these hollowed-out salt rocks are placed

lights to make the salt lamp look more beautiful.

The problem is that when you turn these lamps on inside your home, they absorb and suck away at the chi energy of everybody living there. So, although attractive to look at, they can be dangerous, as they leave you feeling exhausted, lethargic, and devoid of energy.

Activate good mountain stars with crystals 68

When you activate lucky mountain star corners of your home using crystals, it is important to know a little about using crystals for feng shui purposes. For a start, reject all crystals that have been reshaped into sharp points. These can signify secret poison arrows and because they are made from crystals they are doubly powerful in their pernicious effects. Unless you know how to use pointed crystals, it is best not to display them around your home.

Selecting crystals

The best crystals are natural quartz types that appear in an untouched state. Such crystals contain much power. Place them in earth corners Southwest or Northeast or, better still, in corners that enjoy auspicious mountain stars. Having said that, artificial crystals, especially those with a lot of lead, are very brilliant and also acceptable for feng shui purposes.

PROJECT

Crystal balls

It is also an excellent idea to introduce perfect spheres made of solid crystal into your home. Displaying a solid crystal as large as you can afford creates concentrated earth energy within your home. So six round crystal balls inside the house bring excellent period 8 feng shui. But it is also acceptable to place many more of these crystal globes (in assorted colors and of different semi-precious gemstones) if you particularly like them.

Six crystal balls bring excellent earth energy.

Natural rock crystals bring in auspicious mountain energy. Amethyst cluster (left); citrine cluster (center); natural quartz cluster (right).

They are not as powerful as natural crystals because their chi energy is recent, but they do work effectively.

What you really do not want are faded-looking crystals. Instead, always look for bright, sparkling types filled with powerful and precious yang energy. So, the more glitter and sparkle they have, the better they are in attracting great feng shui into the house.

69 Use Chinese art paintings to activate mountain stars

If you prefer, you can use Chinese art paintings depicting mountains to simulate the presence of mountains in sectors or on walls that are affected by the auspicious mountain star 8, 6, or 1. These are the three numbers that signify that the mountain star is lucky.

Activating the sector in your home that is influenced by these mountain star numbers will bring you happiness and excellent relationships, ones in which you will make each other very happy. Just make certain that your mountain painting shows vast, soaring, friendly mountains that are colored with different shades of green. Barren-looking mountains are said to be more bad news than they are worth. So a verdant mountain scene that takes your breath away is the perfect type of painting. It is also better if there is no sign of a water feature in the painting.

When choosing art, opt for lush mountain scenes but avoid water, as this can negate the earth energy symbolized by mountains.

70 When good mountain stars are imprisoned, goodwill is locked up

Corners of the home that have auspicious mountain star numbers should, as far as possible, be kept open and free of clutter, so that chi energy can flow freely. This allows the goodwill chi emanating from the intangible mountain star energies to spread and flow to other corners of the home. Ideally, do not have a large closet or storeroom in the relevant corner, as effectively this keeps all the good luck locked up. If you have a large piece of furniture with locks in this corner, you should relocate it elsewhere in the home. Corners that feature good mountain stars are excellent places to position beds, sofas, and dining tables and chairs.

Different ways to activate mountain stars 71

There are numerous different ways to activate the auspicious mountain stars and the method you choose is entirely a matter of personal preference. Not everyone likes crystals, for example, and Chinese brush paintings of mountains are not exactly everyone's cup of tea. But the important thing to note is that unless you activate an auspicious mountain star as suggested, you will not enjoy the luck brought to that corner of your home. It does not matter how you activate the corner, but you must activate it to feel the full benefits of the auspicious mountain star.

Activating the mountain star

There are many ways to activate an auspicious mountain star (such as a mountain star that has the number 8, 6, or 1), but the best way is to create or simulate mountain earth energy. Therefore, try one of the following suggestions:

• Hang a painting of mountains.

• Build a brick wall.

• Create a pile of rocks.

• Display a collection of crystal.

• Construct a decorative room divider.

Hang a photograph or a painting of mountains to magnify auspicious earth energy.

Build a decorative rock pile to represent good mountain energy in the sectors of your home that feature auspicious mountain "stars" or numbers.

Construct and display a decorative room divider to create a structure with height, symbolizing the might of mountain energy in your home.

72   Afflicted mountain stars result in severe relationship problems

where there is a good mountain star, because this is interpreted as the mountain star falling into water, which suppresses the good attributes of the mountain star's lucky number. When the mountain star has unlucky numbers, introduce objects that suggest an element that exhausts the mountain star's unlucky number. For example, if the unlucky number is 2, use metal energy such as windchimes; if it is 3, use a red triangle or anything that suggests fire energy. If the number is 5, use a five-element pagoda (see Tip 50).

When good mountain star numbers are afflicted – when they are located in corners of the home affected by secret poison arrows, such as physical blockages – it is vital to take action. Mountain stars that are hit by physical afflictions will always result in residents suffering severe relationship strains and disharmony. One problem after another will become apparent, unless you guard every one of your auspicious mountain stars. So check for poison arrows in the areas of your home where mountain stars, or numbers, occur.

In feng shui, mountain stars stand for relationship luck.

Check out the elements

When a mountain star looks like it may be auspicious, it is important that you do not harm or afflict it in any way by including the wrong elements in the sector of the home in which it occurs. Therefore, it is best not to have a sunken water feature in the corner

Check that your good mountain-star sectors are not being afflicted by poison arrows – structures such as high-rise buildings that create invisible direct lines to your home.

When a good mountain star falls into a hole, problems arise   73

A problem that occurs in many homes is when an auspicious mountain star "falls into a hole." An example of this type of situation might be an auspicious mountain star occurring in the part of the garden that also contains a hole, pond, or pool. The best thing to do is close up the hole if at all possible. If the auspicious mountain star occurs where the land is lower than the rest of the garden, that, too, is a bad indicator.

Water features

Take note that ponds, pools, and the like are generally regarded as being holes in the ground, and that this type of feature always has the power to sap a good mountain star of its strength. The result of this happening is that you will experience problems relating to anger and animosity, and you may also find that your health suffers.

Pools curtail the luck of mountain stars   74

A s holes are the nemesis of mountains, it follows that the presence of ponds and pools can pose a threat to auspicious mountain stars. Holes curtail all the luck that is related to your health, longevity, and relationships.

Waterfalls can be lucky

However, if there is a waterfall-type feature, then the water on its own will not harm the

Even a small pool of water, such as a tub collecting rain water or a natural pond in your garden, counts as a water feature. Be sure that it does not reside near a lucky mountain sector.

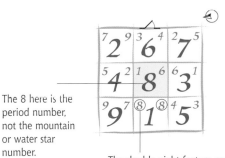

The 8 here is the period number, not the mountain or water star number.

The double-eight feature means the mountain and water star each have the lucky number 8, offering the potential for wealth and relationship luck to be activated.

mountain star. In fact, whenever there is a waterfall, it activates both the mountain and the water star and it is, therefore, excellent for those whose mountain and water stars both have the 8, creating an extremely auspicious double-8 feature. If your house has this combination of lucky water and mountain stars either in the front or at the back of the home, then a waterfall would be the perfect feature to include in the garden.

75   Suppressing bad mountain stars protects the harmony of the home

fatal – hang an all-metal, six-rod windchime in the afflicted corner. This windchime should come with a brass talisman coin with the 12 animals on one side and the Pa Kua with early heaven trigrams on the other.

Use fire to overcome anger

To overcome the number 3 – which brings hostility, anger, misunderstandings, and quarrels – use fire energy. Color the afflicted part of the room red, install bright lights, or place red-colored scatter cushions there. You could also have a red carpet or hang a predominantly red-colored painting there.

Use a pagoda to deflect bad luck

To overcome the number 5 mountain star – which brings overall misfortune luck to all your relationships – place a five-element pagoda in that corner. This is an extremely efficient remedy for this powerful affliction.

Dark reds, oranges, or pinks symbolize fire energy which overcomes the hostility star number 3.

It is crucial to suppress all the bad mountain stars of your home – these are the mountain stars that have the numbers 2, 3, 5, and 7. These numbers create havoc in all your relationships, but to remedy the situation, here are the steps you need to follow:

Use a windchime to guard against ill-health

To overcome the number 2 mountain star – which brings ill-health or the sudden onset of sickness that could, eventually, even prove

Use water to stay safe

To overcome the mountain star 7 – which brings robbery and the ill-luck of being cheated – place an urn of water in the afflicted corner and use plants or fish to transform it into a yang water feature.

Lucky water stars bring enhanced income luck   76

Activating auspicious water stars for wealth luck is one of the most popular aspects of the flying star method of feng shui. It works every time, but to get this technique to enhance your prosperity luck, you will have to be very accurate in assessing the location of your auspicious water stars.

Always use a compass to detect your house facing direction, because it is only when you have ascertained the facing direction of your house correctly that you will be able to select the flying star chart that applies to it. After doing this, it is a matter of superimposing the relevant chart onto a plan of your house layout to orientate you in the correct direction (see Tips 37–42 and 57)

Water numbers equal wealth potential on a flying star chart (see below).

Auspicious water stars are 1, 4, 6, 8, and 9.

The auspicious water star worldwide

Finding the auspicious water star to activate is a method of feng shui that applies equally well to all the countries of the world – to those residing in the northern as well as in the southern hemispheres. There is no difference at all in the use of the directions and the charts. The flying star chart applies to your home in exactly the same way everywhere. Just remember not to estimate or guess at the compass direction. For accurate results, always take a compass reading.

Q & A

Q: *Do the numbers of the flying star charts all apply equally in countries in the northern and southern hemispheres?*
A: Very definitely so. Over the past ten years or so there has been a misconception in southern hemisphere countries such as Australia and South Africa that the application of compass formula feng shui required the directions to be flipped once you crossed the equator – in other words, South would refer to North and East would refer to West. As a result, those who followed this line of reasoning experienced negative effects from their feng shui practice. The charts and numbers apply and work in exactly the same way no matter where you are.

77 Locate the water star 8 in your home to be rich

If you want to become seriously wealthy and have your business take the leap from small-time enterprise to big-time corporation, look for the place of the water star 8 in your home. This can be described as the ultimate wealth spot of your house and it is the location that benefits from the presence of physical water. If you live in an apartment, invest in one of those interior water features that are so popular these days. Remember that in the home it is not necessary to use the rolling-ball variety of water feature. These are better in stores and other retail outlets, as they increase sales turnover. For the home, it is better to look for a wide-brimmed bowl-like container within which you can place water and then activate it with yang-inducing chi energy created by plants and fish.

Gardens

Those who live in houses should activate their gardens – at least, the part of the garden that corresponds to the place of the water star 8.

- For this to be really successful, I always recommend digging a hole in the ground to accommodate a fishpond or swimming pool.

- Remember the annual taboos (see Tip 43), and avoid the directions where digging is dangerous when creating your "hole of prosperity".

- Finally, make sure that there is an opening, such as a window or door, through which chi energy can enter.

PROJECT

A garden water feature

Once you have located the auspicious water star 8 in your garden, you can build a pond or a pool as shown here. Placing a dragon near the water will enhance the power of the water feature.

The water star 8 is better in front of the house than behind it   78

It is always better to have the water star 8 fly to the front of the house than to the back, as the rules of feng shui always encourage the presence of water in front of the entrance. A view of water that can be seen from the house is generally almost always excellent feng shui, so when the water star 8 is also located in the front of the building you have a double bonanza. And according to Taoist feng shui, it is the concept of double goodness that multiplies good fortune.

Encouraging the water star

So, if you can, always try to "bring" the water star 8 to the front of the house. To do this it is necessary to tilt the front door in such a way that it is rebuilt at an angle to the front wall. This usually succeeds in bringing the water star 8 from the back to the front. You can tilt the door by as much as 45° to the left or right to form a castle gate door (see Tip 4). In feng shui, this type of door is also said to attract wealth luck, especially to those who are engaged in commerce.

Water strengthens wealth luck of water stars   79

It is the physical presence of water that energizes the auspicious-numbered water stars, and although the water star 8 is the strongest and most powerful of them all, there are other beneficial numbers. Apart from 8, the most auspicious water star is 9 – this is because it signifies future prosperity. When you activate both water stars 8 and 9, your prosperity luck will last a long time.

After the number 9 comes the number 1, which also stands for water. The water star 1 should be activated with a small water feature. It is up to you how many water features you have, as water in small amounts does not do any harm. Be careful, however, not to have too many large water features, as you should never overdo the energizing effect of water.

It is important that water feature does not overpower a property – this pool, for example, is a little too large for the house.

80 The special energy of swimming pools

A swimming pool is an example of a large water feature that can, potentially, bring you excellent wealth luck. However, it is imperative that your pool is in proportion with your house. This means that a swimming pool should never be so large that it appears to overwhelm the property. If you are able to install a swimming pool in the correct garden location – in the sector of your garden where the water star 8 resides – then it will bring you amazing wealth luck. It will do this even if your pool is small in relation to your house, which is a common problem when houses have been extended over a period of years but the pool has not been enlarged.

Regardless of the size of your swimming pool, to make the most of its special energy you must also have an opening nearby – such as a door or a window in the house – to welcome in the auspicious water energy.

Yang water

It is also important that the pool should never, at any time of the day, look stagnant. It should look like a pool of yang water – this is water that is always moving – so a small fountain or waterfall is a beneficial feature. In addition, note that the water should appear to be flowing in the direction of the house door. Water in front of the house should never appear to be flowing away from the house – it should always flow toward it. This is a small, but vital, point you must bear in mind when using water to activate wealth luck.

Swimming pools can bring wealth energy into your home. If you can, try to create a ripple effect so that the water appears to be flowing toward the house rather than away from it.

A clean and frolicking carp pond brings abundance   81

Instead of a swimming pool you could always install a small fishpond, filling it with auspicious carp. These fish, in feng shui terms, signify an abundance of wealth luck. When a carp pond is located in the place of the water star 8, the fish will bring abundance. This is because in feng shui lore, the word "fish" stands for abundance, and so when they are swimming happily in the place of the water star 8, they create yang energy, and this brings an abundance of prosperity.

Keep your fish healthy and happy

It is important that the carp are healthy and happy, constantly frolicking in the water. Those living in temperate climates should arrange for the pond to be heated in the winter season. Carp cannot usually withstand extreme temperatures. There should also be a filtration system large enough to keep the pond scrupulously clean. There is nothing worse than having a murky, dirty fishpond in front of your house. Bad, dirty water is worse than having no water at all, and sickly fish are worse than having no fish. If you decide to keep fish for feng shui reasons (or for any other) you should learn something about how to look after them properly. When your fish do not survive, it can be very demoralizing, and the chi energy they emit while sick can be negative.

Carp are loved by the Chinese. Healthy carp bring yang energy and prosperity.

82 Exhausting the energy of bad water stars

When water star numbers are negative and bad, it is necessary to exhaust their chi. If you do not do this, they will cause you to lose money and suffer other financial loss. Negative water stars are those with numbers 5, 2, 7, and 3. If your luck is afflicted by these negative water stars, follow the advice below.

Countering money problems

• **The water star 5** is said to be afflicted by the malicious 5 yellow, which brings financial loss. To overcome the effect of the 5 yellow on your wealth luck, you should display plenty of large-sized metallic coins, as the presence of metal will exhaust the earth energy of the 5.

• **The water star 2** brings financial worries and stress brought on by money problems. To overcome these effects, use windchimes or six large, metallic coins. You can also overcome the water star 2 with an image of

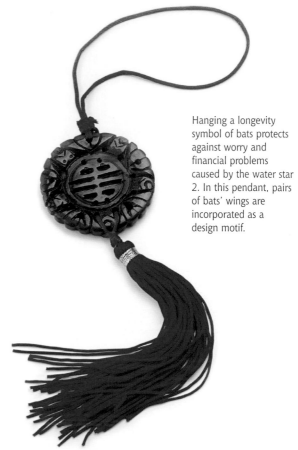

Hanging a longevity symbol of bats protects against worry and financial problems caused by the water star 2. In this pendant, pairs of bats' wings are incorporated as a design motif.

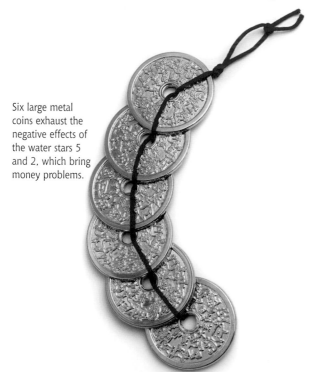

Six large metal coins exhaust the negative effects of the water stars 5 and 2, which bring money problems.

five bats around a longevity symbol – you can find this on a plaque or as a pendant (shown above). This will alleviate your financial worries.

• **The water star 7** either causes your money to be stolen, or it can bring people into your life who will cheat you. To prevent this from happening, you should install a small water feature in the sector of your home where the water star 7 appears.

• **The water star 3** causes you to have legal disputes concerning money matters. This is a very aggravating situation, one that is not at all pleasant, and to overcome the bad energy you should keep the corner afflicted by the water star 3 bright and well lit. Refrain from turning off the light, as fire energy will exhaust the wood energy of the water star 3.

When good water and mountain stars occur together, build a waterfall   83

In some of the flying star charts for period 7 and period 8 (see Tips 37 and 38), there are houses where both the mountain and water stars are equally auspicious – for example, when the number 8 occurs as both the water and mountain stars. This often suggests that residents have to choose whether they wish to activate for wealth (using water) or for relationships (using mountain symbolism). Obviously, both types of luck are equally good and just as important.

The best of both elements

If you find it difficult to decide which to choose, then invest some money and a little effort in building a waterfall. The presence of a waterfall activates both the mountain and the water energy together.

Activating the luck

When the double 8 water and mountain stars occur in the front of the house, near the main door, then you should build the waterfall in front of the main door in the garden. Do not, however, build the waterfall to the right side of the door to the garden (when you are inside looking out). This could cause the man of the house to develop a roving eye, which is not conducive to a happy, harmonious home – for more on this, see Tip 7.

When the double 8 water and mountain stars are behind the house, then ideally the waterfall should also be behind the house. It is important, however, to have an opening, such as a door or a window, close by the waterfall so that beneficial chi can enter the house.

A waterfall need not be grand – a simple arrangement of stones can capture the good water and mountain energy.

84 Keep bad luck water stars locked up

A cabinet located where bad water stars occur in your home locks up the back luck.

One method of keeping the bad water stars under control is simply to lock them up. You can do this by locating a storeroom in the sector where the bad water star occurs. Often, however, it is not possible to alter the function of existing rooms or to change the layout of your home, but you can still take action – by placing a large cabinet in the afflicted sector. In the old days in China, special cabinets were designed exactly for this purpose. Once the negative water stars are locked up, their impact on the residents of the home is considerably diminished.

85 A six-level waterfall unifies the energies of heaven and earth

One of the best-kept secrets when it comes to building an artificial water feature is the six-level waterfall. This design of water feature is excellent for activating the double 8 in the flying star chart – this is where the mountain and water stars are both 8. The waterfall signifies the unity of heaven and earth, and when you place it near an opening into the house it also brings in the energy of the humankind. This coming together of the trinity of heaven, earth, and humankind is what excellent feng shui is about.

The six tiers for the water to cascade down are significant because the number 6 signifies heaven, while the downward-flowing energy signifies earth. In the broader landscape, water tumbles down the mountains bringing wealth and happiness to the people living below. If you wish, you can keep fish inside the collecting pond at the base of the waterfall. Otherwise, you might want to consider introducing plants and water lilies.

A six-level waterfall symbolizes the energy of heaven, earth, and mankind in harmony.

Create a "pure land pond" for family harmony 86

Do what I do and create a "pure land pond" – this is a pond created for the sole purpose of saving the tiny fish that you can buy from fish-keeping stores. These are usually weak, imperfect fish stocked as live food for the types of fancy fish that are kept and bred for their beauty and auspicious meaning. In the East, an example of this is the arrowana, which is also known as the dragon fish. People who keep arrowana for luck are tempted to feed them live fish, rather than training their arrowana to eat fish pellets instead.

Stocking your land pond

Buy several bags of these unfortunate little fish on an auspicious day and free them all into your pure land pond. The fish will surprise you by creating happy water energy inside the pond and within a few months they will have grown into sizeable, colorful fish. My pure land pond is filled with several generations of goldfish. They bring enormous good luck, of course, since the very act of saving these little creatures creates good karma. Moreover, this is one of the best ways of creating the good vibes that promote family harmony.

Rescuing the tiny fish that are sold as feed for other types of fish creates positive energy and good family relationships.

87 Place a dragon image near your water feature for added effectiveness

This not a very well known feng shui secret, but if you want your water features to have added effect then you should discreetly place some dragons near the water's edge, or even inside the water. Not real dragons, of course, but you can select from metal, marble, or coral ones of any size and in any posture. As long as they appear happy – "the thirsty dragon quenches his thirst" – the presence of the dragon empowers the water with the energy of the dragon's lair. It is this that produces the positive chi required to activate the water.

The presence of a dragon near yang water gives your water feature more power and energy.

88 Place tortoises in the North for protection

If you are considering having a water feature such as a pond, a waterfall, or just a small urn filled with water, and the feature is to occupy the North corner of your home, it is a good idea to include a pair of tortoise or terrapin statuettes.

To the Chinese, the tortoise is widely regarded as one of the most benevolent of the celestial creatures. It protects and supports you and your ideas, and it also represents longevity. It is very beneficial for every home to have at least one image of the tortoise. Many feng shui masters even believe that the tortoise image is as powerful, if not more so, than the dragon. In view of this, sometime during the last Ching dynasty there appeared the image of the dragon tortoise – said to combine the support

The dragon tortoise embodies the power of the tortoise and the dragon.

The tortoise symbolizes support.

and strength of the tortoise with the courage and bravado of the dragon. Together, these two creatures create powerful feng shui, so placing a dragon tortoise image near the water features in your home and garden is regarded as enormously auspicious.

The eight-mansions Kua formula of feng shui   89

The eight-mansions method of feng shui categorizes houses according to whether they are East group or West group. East-group houses face North, South, East, or Southeast; West-group houses face West, Southwest, Northwest, and Northeast.

Finding your group

Those familiar with this method of feng shui know that it also classifies people according to whether they are East- or West-group people, and this is based on their Kua number. This number is determined by your gender and lunar year of birth (see Tip 19).

East or West group?

To calculate your Kua number, add the last two digits of your year of birth together and keep adding until you get a single-digit number. Then, for men, deduct this number from 10 and the result is your Kua number; for women, add 5 to this total, and the result is your Kua number (see Tip 19).

Kua numbers	Group	Lucky directions
1, 3, 4, 9	East	North, South, East, Southeast
2, 5, 6, 7, 8	West	West, Northwest, Southwest, Northeast

Commit your Kua number to memory so you don't forget to capture your auspicious directions at all times. It will make a world of difference to your personalized feng shui. All that is required of you is always to remember to sit, chat, talk, negotiate, give a speech, eat, and sleep facing one of the four directions that corresponds to your personal (East or West) group. In the bedroom, as long as you sleep with your head pointed to one of your good directions, you are certain to enjoy good sleeping feng shui. So always take note of the East- and the West-group directions.

Always try to sit facing one of your lucky directions when you are working, eating, and even watching TV. For good family relationships, sleep with your head pointing toward your lucky nien yen direction (see Tip 19).

90 The eight-mansions house luck map

The eight-mansions formula (see Tips 19 and 91) is not just a personalized formula – it also reveals the luck distribution in any home. Every building can be categorized as one of eight types of house, based on its facing direction. Usually this also means the facing direction of the main door, but if the main door is a side door, then generally it is the facing direction of the house gate or place of most yang energy (see Tip 3).

Using the chart

The eight-mansions chart shows which sectors of the house enjoy the four types of good luck and the four types of bad luck (see right).

Based on your house facing direction, you can identify the eight-mansion chart that applies to your home. Select the correct chart and superimpose it on a floor plan to identify the good- and bad-luck sectors. The next eight Tips show you which chart applies to each of

If you work from home, it's important to check that your office falls in a lucky sector and, if not, use remedies to counteract any negative energy.

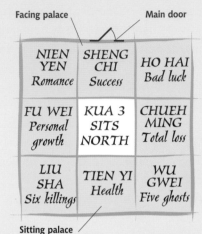

The Eight Mansions luck map

Facing palace — Main door

NIEN YEN Romance	SHENG CHI Success	HO HAI Bad luck
FU WEI Personal growth	KUA 3 SITS NORTH	CHUEH MING Total loss
LIU SHA Six killings	TIEN YI Health	WU GWEI Five ghosts

Sitting palace

The four types of good luck are:

1 **Sheng chi**: prosperity, growth, expansion, success, and wealth.

2 **Nien yen**: marriage, relationships, romance, love, and family.

3 **Tien yi**: good health, wellness, and freedom from illness.

4 **Fu wei**: personal development and enhancement.

The four types of bad luck are:

1 **Ho hai**: mild bad luck, accidents, and similar events.

2 **Wu gwei**, which means five ghosts – people who wish to harm you.

3 **Lui shar**, which means six killings or six types of bad luck

4 **Chueh ming**: total loss and huge misfortune.

the eight facing directions, so all you need do is read the section that applies to you to discover how to improve each bad-luck sector. In this respect, note that it is always the facing palace and sitting palace, or areas, that exert the most influence on the luck of residents. Usually, the facing palace is front center and the sitting palace is back center, as shown.

Optimizing the sectors in a South-facing house 91

A South-facing house is described as sitting North and facing South. Shown here is the eight-mansions chart of a house that faces South. Note that the sheng chi luck resides in the facing palace, or in the South sector of the house. Please note that sheng chi luck is regarded as belonging to the wood element, so wood flying into the South becomes exhausted by the fire energy of the South. Unless the wood energy of this part of the house is strengthened with the presence of water, the sheng chi luck that brings prosperity and success to residents will be curtailed. Thus, it is a good idea to place a water feature in the facing palace of this house. As for the other sectors, the analysis is as follows:

Wood in the South sector of a South-facing house brings luck, but it must be strengthened by the water element, such as an auspicious water feature.

Analyzing South-facing house luck

Romance luck, metal, flies into the Southeast, wood. Here, the romance star is strong, so there is no need to do anything here.

Personal growth luck, wood chi, flies into the East, also wood – so here wood is strengthened. There is no need to do anything, but do not have too much wood here as this causes over-competitiveness.

Six killings belongs to the water element, and when it flies into the Northeast, earth, it is pressed down by earth energy. There is no need to do anything as the six killings is therefore kept under control.

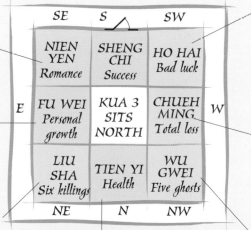

Bad luck ho hai is earth chi, and by flying into the Southwest its bad luck chi is strengthened. So this house needs metal energy here to exhaust the bad luck.

Chueh ming, or total loss luck, is metal chi, and flying into the West, which is also metal, strengthens it. So water energy is needed here to exhaust the bad luck.

The sitting palace (North) has good health luck. Here, earth chi flies into water so good health luck is distracted. Fire energy will strengthen earth and bring better health.

Wu gwei has fire energy, and by flying into the Northwest, metal, it is strengthened. Five ghosts' luck needs to be pressed down and exhausted, so place earth energy, such as crystals, in this sector.

92   Making the most of a North-facing house

The North sector of a North-facing house – here, the front door sector – has natural good luck, which you can enhance with a water feature.

A North-facing house is described as sitting South and facing North. Shown here is the eight-mansions chart of a house that faces North. Note that the sheng chi luck resides in the facing palace, or the North sector of the house. Since sheng chi luck belongs to the wood element, wood flying into the North sector becomes strengthened by the water energy of the North. So, the presence of water here expands the sheng chi luck, which brings prosperity and success to the residents of this house. So it is a good idea to place a water feature in the facing palace of this house, or do nothing at all as it is already lucky enough. As for the other sectors of the house, the analysis is as follows:

Analyzing North-facing house luck

Bad luck is earth chi which flies into the Northwest, metal. Here, the bad luck chi will be naturally exhausted, so there is no need to do anything.

Six killings chi belongs to the water element, and when it flies to the West sector, metal, it expands. Exhaust the water element by using lots of wood energy, so place plants here.

Five ghosts belongs to fire energy and by flying into the Southwest, earth, it is exhausted. There is no need to do anything further.

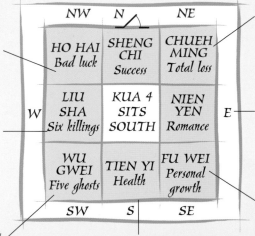

	NW N	NE
	HO HAI *Bad luck* SHENG CHI *Success*	CHUEH MING *Total loss*
W	LIU SHA *Six killings* KUA 4 SITS SOUTH NIEN YEN *Romance*	E
	WU GWEI *Five ghosts* TIEN YI *Health* FU WEI *Personal growth*	
	SW S	SE

Total loss luck is metal chi, and by flying into the Northeast, which is earth, it is considerably strengthened. So you need to use water energy to exhaust the bad luck here.

Romance luck metal flies into East, which is wood. Here the romance star nien yen, metal, is strong, so there is no need to do anything.

Personal growth luck, which is wood chi, flies into the Southeast, also wood. So here wood is strengthened and there is no need to do anything. Avoid too much wood here, however, or the energy becomes over-competitive.

The sitting palace (South) has good health luck. Here, tien yi earth chi flies into a fire element sector, so the good health of residents is enhanced. There is no need to do anything more.

Adjusting the energies of a West-facing house 93

A West-facing house is described as sitting East and facing West. Shown here is the eight-mansions chart of a house that faces West. Note once again that the sheng chi luck resides in the facing palace, or the West sector of the house. Since sheng chi luck belongs to the wood element, wood flying into the West sector is destroyed by the metal energy of the West. So, the presence of water here is vital as it expands the sheng chi luck, which brings prosperity and success while, at the same time, weakening and exhausting the metal that hurts the sheng chi. So placing water at the front of the house will greatly improve its prosperity luck. As for the other sectors, the analysis is as follows:

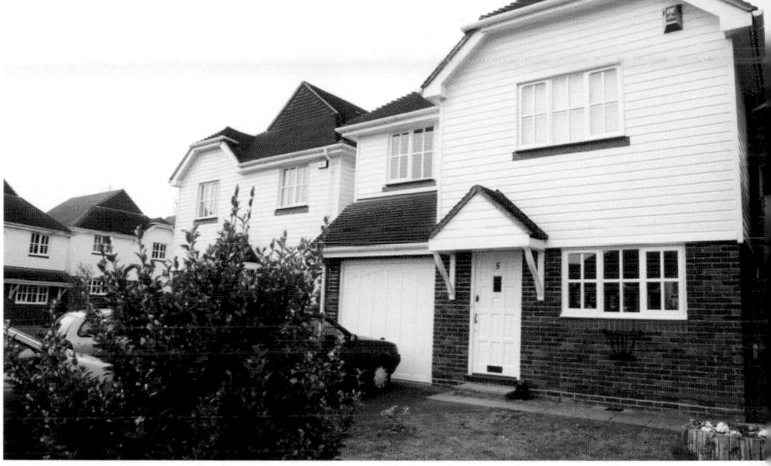

The element of success luck, sheng chi, is wood, but the metal element of the West sector of a West-facing house exhausts it, so display a water feature to strengthen wood.

Analyzing West-facing house luck

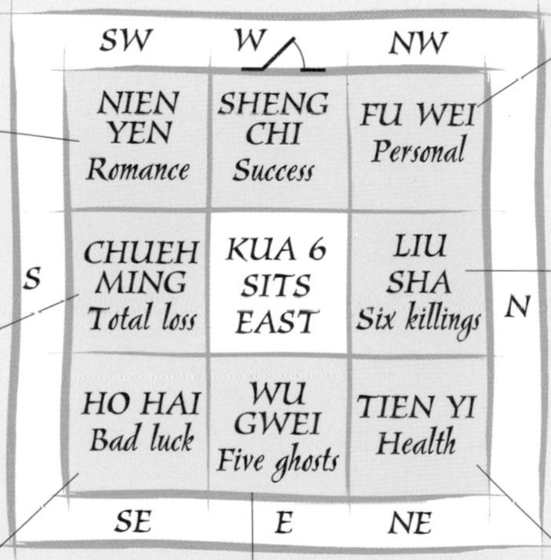
SW
W
NW
NIEN YEN
Romance
SHENG CHI
Success
FU WEI
Personal
S
CHUEH MING
Total loss
KUA 6 SITS EAST
LIU SHA
Six killings
N
HO HAI
Bad luck
WU GWEI
Five ghosts
TIEN YI
Health
SE
E
NE

Romance luck metal flies to the Southwest, which is earth. Here, the romance star, metal, is strengthened by the earth energy of the sector so there is no need to do anything, except place love symbols to stimulate romance luck.

Total loss luck, metal chi, is destroyed when it flies into the fire of the South. So you do not need to do anything here.

Bad luck ho hai is earth chi, and by flying into the Southeast, which is wood, it is destroyed by the wood chi. There is no need to do anything more.

The sitting palace (East) has five ghosts' luck and fire energy, enhanced by the sector's wood energy. Place earth here to exhaust the fire energy, such as boulders or crystals, and avoid a great deal of aggravation.

Personal growth luck, which is wood chi, flies into the Northwest, which is metal, destroying wood. Place water here to strengthen personal growth luck while exhausting the metal luck of the sector.

Six killings chi has the water element and when it flies to the North water sector, it is expanded. Exhaust water with lots of wood energy, so place plants here.

Good health luck has the earth element and is in the Northeast sector, which is also earth, so there is no need to do anything further. This home's residents will enjoy good health.

94   Creating balance and harmony in an East-facing house

An East-facing house is described as sitting West and facing East. Shown here is the eight-mansions chart of a house that faces East. Note that the sheng chi luck resides in the facing palace, the East sector of the house. Since sheng chi luck belongs to the wood element, wood flying into the East sector is strengthened by the wood energy of the East. So the sheng chi luck, which brings prosperity and success to residents of this house, is enhanced. As for the other sectors, the analysis is as shown below.

The East sector of an East-facing house is lucky because it shares its wood element with sheng chi success luck.

Analyzing East-facing house luck

Tien yi luck, which brings good health and belongs to the earth element, is in the Southeast sector, which is wood. Here, earth is dominant and it is a good idea to include fire element energizers if you wish to improve the health luck of residents.

Bad luck ho hai is earth chi, and by flying into the Northeast, which is earth, it is strengthened. As a result it is a good idea to place metal element energizers here to exhaust the bad luck earth energy.

Romance luck metal flies into the North, which is water. Here the romance star, nien yen, metal, is exhausted by the water energy of the sector, so place additional earth elements here to strengthen the love and romance luck.

Personal growth luck, which is wood chi, is exhausted by the fire chi of the South. To strengthen wood and destroy fire energy, place water in this sector .

NE	E	SE
HO HAI *Bad luck*	SHENG CHI *Success*	TIEN YI *Health*
NIEN YEN *Romance*	KUA 9 SITS WEST	FU WEI *Personal growth*
CHUEH MING *Total loss*	WU GWEI *Five ghosts*	LIU SHA *Six killings*
NW	W	SW

N (left)   S (right)

Total loss luck has metal chi and by flying into the Northwest, which is metal, it is strengthened. It is very important to place a water feature in this sector to exhaust the metal element and protect the patriarch of the family from total loss bad chi.

The sitting palace (West) has five ghosts' luck. Here, the five ghosts' fire energy is distracted by the metal energy of the sector, which it destroys. Introduce additional earth elements, such as crystals and boulders, to distract the five ghosts.

Six killings chi belongs to the water element, and when it flies to the Southwest, which is earth, the six killings' luck is destroyed. So it is not necessary to do anything more.

Capturing success sheng chi in a Southwest-facing house   95

A Southwest-facing house is described as sitting Northeast and facing Southwest. Shown here is the eight-mansions chart of a house that faces Southwest. Note that the sheng chi luck resides in the facing palace, the Southwest sector of the house. Since sheng chi luck belongs to the wood element, wood flying into the Southwest sector destroys earth, the element there. It is a good idea to place water in this sector to strengthen the sheng chi luck. As for the other sectors, the analysis is as follows:

Analyzing Southwest-facing house luck

Romance luck metal flies into the West, which is metal. Here the romance star, nien yen, metal is strong, so there is no need to do anything for this sector.

Health luck, tien yi, which is earth chi, flies into the Northwest, which is metal. So here, earth is exhausted by metal. Strengthen the health luck with extra fire energy. Install a bright light in this sector to safeguard residents' health luck.

Bad luck has earth-element chi, which is strengthened in the fiery South. Install a remedy using metal energy to exhaust the earth chi of ho hai. Hang windchimes with six rods to dispel the bad luck.

Total loss luck is metal chi and by flying into the Southeast, which is wood, it becomes distracted. Exhaust the bad luck of chueh ming by placing water here.

	S	SW	W	
	HO HAI *Bad luck*	SHENG CHI *Success*	NIEN YEN *Romance*	
SE	CHUEH MING *Total loss*	KUA 5/8 SITS NE	TIEN YI *Health*	NW
	LIU SHA *Six killings*	FU WEI *Personal growth*	WU GWEI *Five ghosts*	
	E	NE	N	

Six killings chi, with its water element, flies to the East wood sector and is exhausted. There is no need to do anything here.

The sitting palace (Northeast) has personal growth luck. Here wood chi flies into an earth element sector. Further enhance wood with a small water feature.

Wu gwei, or five ghosts' luck, belongs to the fire element. Flying into the North it encounters water, which destroys its fire. There is no need to do anything further.

The element of the Southwest, earth, clashes with the wood element of sheng chi success luck. Water in the Southwest sector boosts wood chi and therefore success luck.

96 Pressing down the bad luck sectors in a Southeast-facing house

A Southeast-facing house is described as sitting Northwest and facing Southeast. Shown here is the eight-mansions chart of a house that faces Southeast. Note that the sheng chi luck resides in the facing palace, the Southeast sector of the house. Since sheng chi luck belongs to the wood element, wood flying into the wood sector is strengthened, which brings prosperity and success to the residents of this house. It is a good idea to place a water feature in the facing palace of this house – or do nothing at all, as it is already lucky enough. As for the other sectors, the analysis is as shown below.

This Southeast-facing house has intrinsic luck, which is helpful for those living in town houses where there is little space at the front of the property for remedies and enhancers such as plants and water features.

Analyzing Southeast-facing house luck

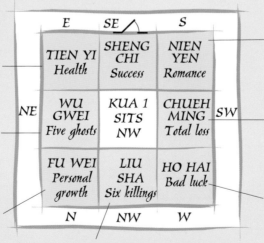

Health luck chi belongs to the earth element and when it flies to the East wood sector it is destroyed by wood. Strengthen the earth element using lots of fire energy – install bright lights here for good health luck.

Five ghosts' luck belongs to fire energy and by flying to the Northeast, earth, it is exhausted. There is no need to do anything further.

Personal growth luck, which is wood chi, flies to the North, which is water. Here wood is strengthened and there is no need to do anything.

Romance luck metal flies to the South, which is fire. Here the romance star, which is metal, is being destroyed, so place earth energy, such as boulders or crystals, here.

Total loss luck is metal chi and by flying to the Southwest, which is earth, it is considerably strengthened. So bring in water energy to exhaust the bad luck of chueh ming.

Bad luck ho hai is earth chi and by flying into the West, metal, it is exhausted, which is a good thing. There is no need to do anything.

The sitting palace (Northwest) has six killings' luck, which belongs to the water element, and is flying into the metal sector. The six killings is strong and must be exhausted by wood, so place plants here.

Chart contents:

	E	SE	S
	TIEN YI Health	SHENG CHI Success	NIEN YEN Romance
NE	WU GWEI Five ghosts	KUA 1 SITS NW	CHUEH MING Total loss	SW
	FU WEI Personal growth	LIU SHA Six killings	HO HAI Bad luck
	N	NW	W

Creating good fortune luck for a Northwest-facing house

ANorthwest-facing house is described as sitting Southeast and facing Northwest. Shown here is the eight-mansions chart of a house that faces Northwest. Note that the sheng chi luck resides in the facing palace, the Northwest sector of the house. Since sheng chi luck belongs to the wood element, wood flying to the Northwest sector is destroyed by the metal of the Northwest. It is necessary to have water here to strengthen the sheng chi luck, which brings prosperity and success to the residents of this house. So placing a water feature in the facing palace is a good idea for this house. As for the other sectors, the analysis is as shown below.

A water feature such as a pool in the Northwest sector of a Northwest-facing house brings wealth to the residents.

Analysing Northwest-facing house luck

Personal growth luck, which is wood chi, flies into the West, where it si destroyed by metal. Place water here to strengthen the fu wei luck while exhausting the sector's metal luck.

Tien yi luck, which brings good health and belongs to the earth element, is in the Southwest sector, also earth. There is no need to do anything, as the residents of this house will enjoy good health.

The five ghosts here is very strong as fire energy overcomes the metal chi of the Northwest. Placing water at the front of the house will reduce the bad effects of the five ghosts chi.

Ho hai bad luck belongs to the earth element and when it flies to the North sector it meets up witn the water element. Exhaust the earth chi with metal energy.

Romance luck, nien yen, metal flies into Northeast, which is earth. Here, the romance star, nien yen, metal is strengthened by the earth energy of the sector, and so there is no need to do anything more except to place love symbols to stimulate romance luck.

Total loss luck is metal chi and by flying into the East, which is wood, it becomes distracted. Exhaust the chueh ming luck by placing a water feature here.

The sitting palace (Southeast) has the six killings' luck. Here the water energy of the six killings is exhausted by the wood energy of the Southeast sector. There is no need to do anything here.

	W	NW	N
	FU WEI *Personal growth*	SHENG CHI *Success*	HO HAI *Bad luck*
SW	TIEN YI *Health*	KUA 7 SITS SE	NIEN YEN *Romance*	NE
	WU GWEI *Five ghosts*	LIU SHA *Six killings*	CHUEH MING *Total loss*
	S	SE	E

98 Optimizing eight-mansion energies in a Northeast-facing house

A Northeast-facing house is described as sitting Southwest and facing Northeast. Shown here is the eight-mansions chart of a house that faces Northeast. Note that the sheng chi luck resides in the facing palace, the Northeast sector of the house. Since sheng chi luck belongs to the wood element, wood flying into the Northeast sector becomes distracted by the earth energy of the Northeast. It needs to be strengthened further and the presence of water here will expand the sheng chi luck. This brings prosperity and success to the residents of the house. It is a good idea to place a water feature in the facing palace of this house. As for the other sectors, the analysis is as follows:

If you cannot introduce a water feature to the Northeast sector of your Northeast-facing home, you can symbolize water by painting your front door blue.

Analysing Northeast-facing house luck

Total loss luck is metal chi and by flying into the North, which is water, it becomes considerably exhausted and weakened. There is no need to do anything more.

Bad luck ho hai is earth chi and is flying into the East, which is wood. Here, the bad luck chi is destroyed, which is a good thing, so there is no need to do anything.

Five ghosts' luck has fire energy and by flying into the Southeast, wood, it is enhanced. Place crystals here to protect residents from harmful people.

Romance luck metal flies into the Northwest, which is metal. Here the romance star, metal, is strong, so there is no need to do anything here.

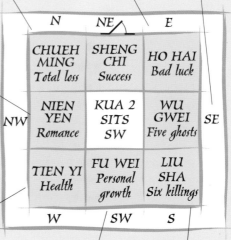

N	NE	E
CHUEH MING *Total loss*	SHENG CHI *Success*	HO HAI *Bad luck*
NIEN YEN *Romance*	KUA 2 SITS SW	WU GWEI *Five ghosts*
TIEN YI *Health*	FU WEI *Personal growth*	LIU SHA *Six killings*

(NW — left, SE — right, W, SW, S — bottom)

Health luck, tien yi, which is wood chi, flies into the west, which is metal. So here wood is destroyed by the metal and needs to be strengthened, otherwise the health of the residents of the house will suffer. Place water here to feed the wood chi. Water also exhausts the harmful metal.

The sitting palace (Southwest) has personal growth luck, whose element is wood. Here wood chi flies into an earth element sector, so the self-development luck of residents still needs strengthening. Place water here to do this.

Six killings chi belongs to the water element, and when it flies to the South fire sector it still needs to be overcome. Exhaust the water element using lots of wood energy, so place plants here.

The powerful influences of flying star specials 99

One of the most exciting aspects of flying star feng shui is the depth of its many indicators of potentially powerful feng shui. Long ago, flying star methods were a closely guarded secret and feng shui masters of the old school would simply leave their clients bewildered by the array of recommendations offered. Seldom were explanations given, with the result that many people were left guessing as to the true reason for changing their door directions, tilting their entrances, or changing the color of their walls. All that was offered were dire warnings of misfortune unless their advice was heeded to the letter. Rare indeed was the 20th-century feng shui master who was patient enough to explain. This is even assuming that he was completely familiar with the esoteric underpinnings of the compass formulas. Most had studied under other masters on an ad hoc basis; few ever attended schools or went through the disciplined scholastic training we are familiar with today.

Modern feng shui

Those who study feng shui today from experienced masters learn best when their knowledge is supplemented by books, through carrying out research, and by practical testing. It is now excitingly possible for almost anyone to have access to the flying star feng shui methods of analyzing and advising on feng shui. If you wish to go deeper into the method, however, it is a good idea to know about the "specials," which refer to the different combinations of numbers that bring extra powerful good fortune. Houses that are converted into period 8 houses will be able to benefit from some amazingly exceptional luck. Listed over the following eight tips are some of the specials. You can either look for a house that demonstrates some of the combinations described, or try to transform your existing house to enjoy the benefits.

Flying star special formulas are based around the energies of the natural world – water and earth, or mountains.

100   Southwest and Northeast-facing houses enjoy auspicious "specials" luck

One of the most exciting discoveries I made while analyzing the period 8 charts a few years ago in preparation for the new period was the amazing good fortune that is awaiting residents of houses enjoying a position oriented on a Southwest/Northeast axis. If you refer to the period charts given earlier (see Tips 38 and 39), you will see that period 8 houses that face Southwest 1 or Northeast 1 will enjoy the sum-of-ten special; while houses that face Southwest 2 or Northeast 2 directions will enjoy the parent-string-combination special. Note that:

Homes that face Southwest or Northeast sit on what is known as the earth axis – the earth element is associated with relationship luck in feng shui.

Does your home benefit from "specials" luck?

Homes facing Northeast 1 and 2/3 and Southwest 1 and 2/3 have special number combinations – see Tips 103 and 104.

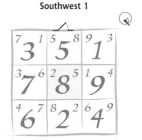

Northeast 1

^{9} 4 ^{6}	^{2} 2 ^{8}	^{7} 6 ^{4}
^{4} 9 ^{1}	^{5} 8 ^{2}	^{6} 7 ^{3}
^{3} 1 ^{9}	^{8} 5 ^{5}	^{1} 3 ^{7}

Southwest 1

^{7} 3 ^{1}	^{5} 5 ^{8}	^{9} 1 ^{3}
^{3} 7 ^{6}	^{2} 8 ^{5}	^{1} 9 ^{4}
^{4} 6 ^{7}	^{8} 2 ^{2}	^{6} 4 ^{9}

Northeast 2/3

^{1} 4 ^{7}	^{8} 2 ^{5}	^{3} 6 ^{9}
^{6} 9 ^{3}	^{5} 8 ^{2}	^{4} 7 ^{1}
^{7} 1 ^{4}	^{2} 5 ^{8}	^{9} 3 ^{6}

Southwest 2/3

^{6} 3 ^{9}	^{8} 5 ^{2}	^{4} 1 ^{7}
^{1} 7 ^{4}	^{2} 8 ^{5}	^{3} 9 ^{6}
^{9} 6 ^{3}	^{5} 2 ^{8}	^{7} 4 ^{1}

- **The sum-of-ten special** brings excellent relationships or wealth luck.

- **The parent string-combination special** brings great good fortune to the family for three generations, or 180 years of continuing good fortune. This happens when the number combination in a square is 1, 4, 7 or 2, 5, 8.

What's the effect of "specials?"

These specials help overcome the monthly and annual aggravations that are brought by individual negative numbers, which is to say that they have the power, ultimately, to overcome whatever affliction the bad star numbers bring. So do check if yours is a Southwest- or a Northeast-facing house and then study the chart that accurately depicts your house in the following Tips.

Mountain star sum-of-ten brings excellent relationship luck 101

You will discover that if your house faces Southwest 1, it will enjoy what is described as the sum-of-ten combinations between the mountain star and the period star. Examine the chart carefully and you will find that every sector has the sum-of-ten combination of numbers.

What's the formula?

In the South sector, the mountain star 7 combines with the period star 3.

In the Southwest, the number 5 combines with the 5, and so on. This type of flying star chart combination of numbers is special because it does not occur often. When your house enjoys this chart, everyone living there will have excellent relationship luck. The people in their lives will bring them good fortune or opportunities for all manner of successes. In addition, the mountain star also brings good health, which means that residents will also enjoy excellent health.

Maximizing your potential

To maximize the potential of such a house, it should ideally have a regular shape – a square or rectangular shape is best. To use the chart, superimpose it onto a plan of the house, using the compass directions as a guide to where to place the numbers of each sector. You will then be able to identify the different star numbers that influence or impact on each sector.

Do note that even though you may enjoy the sum-of-ten special you will still need to remedy any afflictions brought by the negative

Check your home's flying star chart for the sum-of-ten, as shown below, to see if your home will bring you good relationship luck.

A home with great love and health luck

For a house facing Southwest 1

Mountain star 7 combines with period star 3 to equal 10 – meaning that this home brings fantastic relationship luck and good health

7 1	5 8	9 3
3	5	1
3 6	2 5	1 4
7	8	9
4 7	8 2	6 4
6	2	4

stars and enhance the good luck brought by the lucky ones. The specials tell you only that, in the big picture, your house will ultimately bring you good fortune.

102 Water star sum-of-ten brings amazing wealth luck

If your house is facing Northeast 1, then you and your fellow residents will benefit from what is described as the water star sum-of-ten chart, which brings extra-complete wealth luck. Residents are sure to become prosperous and wealthy, and this is the type of wealth that grows and expands. As in the case of the mountain star combination (see Tip 101), houses should have a regular shape to benefit fully from the sum-of-ten special. Thus, if you look closely you will see that, for example, in the Northeast the water star 8 combines with the period star 2 to make 10; and in the sitting palace in the Southwest the 5 combining with 5 also makes 10.

Homes with balanced, more regular shapes benefit best from the sum-of-ten combination, which can bestow excellent wealth luck for all the residents.

Do take note that, while the sum-of-ten does override all other afflictions brought by the intangible negative energy of the chart, it is still a good idea to place individual remedies to overcome the illness star 2, the quarrelsome star 3, and so on when they occur as annual, monthly, water, or mountain stars. These are the aggravations that make daily living very tiresome, so placing remedies in the appropriate sectors of your home will do much to alleviate the situation.

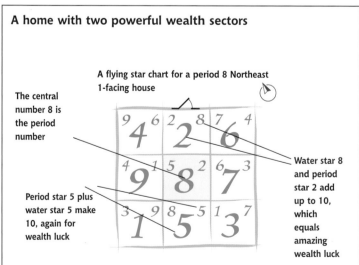

A home with two powerful wealth sectors

A flying star chart for a period 8 Northeast 1-facing house

The central number 8 is the period number

Period star 5 plus water star 5 make 10, again for wealth luck

Water star 8 and period star 2 add up to 10, which equals amazing wealth luck

Looking out for yin spirit formation in the home 103

Another "special" you should be on the lookout for guards against what is referred to as the yin spirit formation in the home – an excess of yin brought about by the presence of too much yin chi. In flying star charts, this means that there are too many yin numbers in the bedrooms of the house. It is therefore necessary to check the numbers that rule each of the bedrooms. You do this by identifying the chart that applies to your house and then superimposing the chart onto a plan layout of your home. If the numbers in the bedroom are all yin numbers, then there is the danger of yin spirit formation, which causes stagnation, loneliness, and general unhappiness sweeping over the residents. Yin spirit is the greatest cause for depression, so it is worthwhile adding plenty of yang energy to act as a balance. The yin numbers are 2, 4, 7, and 9. Counter this with bright lights, moving objects, sounds, and pets. Nothing beats this affliction better than having a pet around.

Numbers 4 and 7 are yin. When these two numbers both occur in the bedroom sector, they can cause depressive energy.

Q & A

Q: *What else can I do to protect my home from depressive energies?*

A: In feng shui, it is vital to guard against what feng shui masters refer to as yin spirit formation in the home generally or in individual rooms. This can happen in many different ways and it can often lead to illness and a weakening of the spirit and energy. To counter this danger, you can use bright lights to create yang energy. Keep the lights turned on or introduce glitter lamps (see right) into afflicted rooms. You can also keep the television turned on to create sounds or keep a fan switched on to create plenty of movement. When you introduce objects into the space that bring "life" then yang energy is automatically created. Having pets is, therefore, another good way to prevent yin spirit formation.

Glitter lamps keep the energy positively yang.

104 Go slow when there is too much yang energy

While there is danger in having too much yin energy (see Tip 103), it is equally bad to have excessive yang energy. The yang numbers are 1, 3, 6, and 8. If you find that any of the bedrooms in your home have a combination of only these numbers, residents of those rooms will suffer from excessive yang energy. When excessive yang occurs, there is too much activity, too much pressure, too many expectations – a situation that needs cooling down. Quarrels and misunderstandings are sure to break out, and sometimes they can become serious.

Creating a cool ambience

The remedy is to introduce the balancing influence of yin energy. The

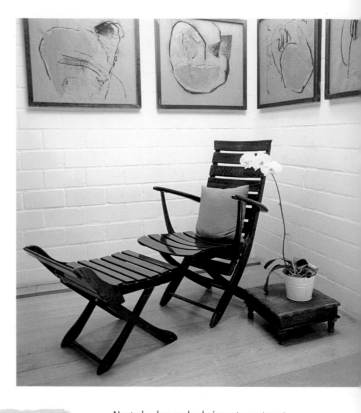

Neutral colors and calming art counteracts overactive yang energy.

best indicator of yin is quietness and stillness. Here are some simple guidelines:

- Reduce the noise level by moving radios and televisions out of the room. Keep the lights dimmed.

- Hang art with soothing colors – this suggests yin chi. Never hang pictures of women in the bedroom as this creates marriage troubles, even though women signify yin energy.

- Declutter – begin with the rooms where arguments most often occur.

Take advantage of the double-8 mountain and water stars   105

All houses facing the cardinal directions of North, South, East, and West will enjoy the double 8 phenomenon – this means that both the water and mountain stars (the small numbers to the left and right of a period number) are 8. This double 8 occurrence is located either in front or at the back of the house, depending on its facing direction.

All houses facing North 1, South 2/3, East 1, and West 1 will experience the double 8 phenomenon in the front of the house in the center palace. These houses will benefit enormously from having a waterfall in front directly facing the front door to activate the double 8 mountain and water stars. Bear in mind that the waterfall signifies the energies of both the mountain and water. Let the flow of the waterfall be gentle and design the feature to have six levels of water flowing down (see Tip 85). Do not build a waterfall that is too large – it must always be in balance with the size of your front door and house.

$_5 7 ^2$	$_2 3 ^9$	$_7 5 ^9$
$_6 6 ^1$	$_4 8 ^3$	$_2 1 ^5$
$_1 2 ^6$	$_⑧ 4 ^8$	$_⑧ 9 ^4$

North, South, East, or West-facing homes' lucky sector is indicated by the location of the double 8s.

Activate the period's direct spirit of the northeast with a mountain   106

Another important special, which is easy for anyone to activate, is to take note of period 8's direct and indirect spirit – these bring up-to-date strong chi energy. Activate the direct spirit, which is located in the Northeast of the home, with mountain symbolism.

The benefits of a mountain

This mountain can be represented by a little mound of stones, boulders, or a real heap of earth. If you live in an apartment, use a crystal geode to simulate the mountain – place it in the Northeast of your home to activate the direct spirit of the period and watch it bring you amazing support luck from all quarters. You can also place a picture or painting of a real mountain range such as the Himalayas on the Northeast wall of your home. This will benefit everyone in your home, but especially the young sons of the family. Doing so will bring you much added income and wealth luck.

Mountain imagery benefits the whole family, especially the sons.

Display crystals to symbolize the good energy of mountains.

107 Energize the period's indirect spirit of the southwest with water

When there is a small pool or pond in the Southwest of your property (preferably in the garden) it activates the indirect spirit of period 8, and this brings wealth luck. It also benefits the matriarch in particular.

You can also activate period 8's indirect spirit by placing water in the Southwest. This is the location of the indirect spirit and placing water here will activate wealth luck for the mother figure of the home. Place a yang water feature here – it can be a pond, a pool, a waterfall, or anything at all that suggests clean, moving water.

The benefits of water

All through period 8, the Southwest corner of your house benefits from the presence of physical water – it does not matter what direction your house faces. This is where water can bring great good fortune. Moreover, if your home is Southwest facing, the Southwest sector is also visited by the very auspicious water star 8 (see the flying star chart in Tip 38). So I always alert everyone to the fantastic potential of all Southwest 1-facing houses. Even if your are an East-group person, if you can, try to find a house that has a Southwest 1-facing orientation and then activate the front of the house by displaying a water feature there.

Feng shui astrology – directions and animal signs 108

A very easy method of practicing instant feng shui astrology is to study the astrology wheel, which shows where each of the 12 Chinese animal signs has its direction. In the Chinese calendar, the animal signs are known as the earthly branches of the year, and they each have a matching compass direction. Thus, depending on your animal sign, you will have a direction location in the house that corresponds to you and your luck.

Finding your direction

Once you find the direction that applies to you personally, you must then ensure that neither a toilet nor a storeroom is located there, otherwise your personal luck will be afflicted. The easiest way to find your direction is to determine your animal sign based on your year of birth (see page 11), then check the astrology

wheel shown here. Note that each animal sign is allotted a 15° segment of the compass direction The four cardinal directions, South, North, East, and West, are represented by one animal sign each – the horse, at, rabbit, and rooster, respectively. The secondary directions, Southwest, Northwest, Southeast, and Northeast, have two animal signs each.

To make the most of this method of optimizing the feng shui of everybody in your home, you should go on to identify the personalized astrological direction of all residents and then neutralize all negative afflictions in those directions while enhancing the relevant corners with the correct energizing symbols.

There are twelve animal signs in the Chinese zodiac: the Rat, Ox, Tiger, Rabbit, Dragon, Snake, Horse, Sheep, Monkey, Rooster, Dog, and Boar. Each occupies 15° of the compass. It is good feng shui to ensure that the direction that corresponds to your sign is neither missing nor afflicted, and instead has many auspicious objects to energize the sector for you.

109 Activate your animal-sign direction to improve personal luck

Once you find the location that corresponds to your animal sign, maximize your luck by strengthening the chi of that area. If there is a toilet or a storeroom occupying this direction, however, do not activate – inside a toilet or storeroom, the chi is afflicted or locked up and is doing you no good at all.

Note the compass direction associated with your animal sign, then place an image of your animal in the corresponding sector of your home. Displaying your animal with gemstones adds to its power to bring you auspicious luck.

Activating your luck

The best way to activate for good things to come into your life is to use energizing images of your own astrological animal sign surrounded by wish-fulfilling jewels, which are cut crystals. It is best to use animal images made from natural crystal, such as quartz, agates, tourmaline, jade, and so forth. These natural treasures from deep within the earth contain very concentrated chi. When surrounded by wish-fulfilling jewels and positioned in your office or on your desk in the direction of your astrology sign, the chi becomes very engaged with your personal energy. Choose crystal colors as follows:

- Yellow cut crystals, cush as citrine, for wealth wishes

- Pink cut crystals, such as ruby or rose quartz, for love-related wishes

- Blue cut crystals, such as blue chalcedony, for healing wishes

- Green cut crystals, such as peridot or emerald for expansion and growth

- Lavender cut crystals, such as amethyst, for personal growth and development.

Finding your astro-compass sector

ANIMAL SIGN	COMPASS BEARING	COMPASS SECTOR
Rat	337.5°–352.5°	North 1
Ox	22.5°–37.5°	Northeast 1
Tiger	37.5°–52.5°	Northeast 2
Rabbit	67.5°–97.5°	East 2
Dragon	112.5°–127.5°	Southeast 1
Snake	142.5°–157.5°	Southeast 3
Horse	172.5°–187.5°	South 2
Sheep	202.5°–217.5°	Southwest 1
Monkey	232.5°–247.5°	Southwest 3
Rooster	262.5°–277.5°	West 2
Dog	292.5°–307.5°	Northwest 1
Boar	322.5°–337.5°	Northwest 3

Astrology allies enhance your social life 110

You can also empower your relationships chi by placing images of your astrology allies and secret friends in your space. This brings the luck of good friends, of mentors, and of helpful people into your life. The identification of your astrology friends and allies is very much part of astrological feng shui. The idea is symbolic, and symbolism is an extremely large part of feng shui practice. All over China, the moment you step foot onto that great country you will see an incredible number of guardian and auspicious symbols. The 12 animal signs are an integral part of the symbolism of astrological feng shui, so familiarize yourself with your affinity triangle of allies and with your secret friend.

The dragon, monkey and rat are equally compatible in Chinese astrology, so they are said to form an affinity triangle.

The affinity triangles of allies

These groupings of animals get along well:

- Snake, rooster, and ox

- Dragon, monkey, and rat

- Horse, tiger, and dog

- Boar, sheep, and rabbit

Friends and allies

Your secret allies are even more amazingly important to you, so also take note of who they are. The chart shown above indicates the kind of chi luck that is created when the pairings of secret friends are displayed according to your signs. You will see that the sheep and horse together indicate the luck of finding a helpful patron. A snake and monkey together bring gambling and speculative luck. A rooster and dragon together bring friends and allies into your life, while a dog and a rabbit attract unexpected windfalls. A tiger and a boar bring a secret friend and, finally, a rat and an ox together bring the luck of harmony.

When you pay attention to energizing your animal signs and your friends and allies, you will discover that:

- Your social life is enhanced in a very positive way.

- You will feel happier and have a wider circle of contacts.

- You life will be full and will not have the usual aggravations. You will find it much easier to interact with other people, and you will also discover allies when you least expect them.

111   Avoid your natural zodiac enemies

You must be very mindful that the astrological wheel also alerts you to your natural astrological foes, and it is imperative you do not display their image in your direction. Thus, for example, the dog and dragon are natural enemies, so it is important not to display the dragon image in the direction that corresponds to that of the dog – in other words, do not place the dragon in the Northwest 1 direction.

However, it would be excellent to draw in the energy of the dragon, which is one of the most auspicious of symbols, into your house. To do this, place the dragon in his own direction of the Southeast – or you can also have the dragon in the East or in the North. In any case, the dragon is a special circumstance as he is so powerful.

Those born in the dog year should also be aware that it is perfectly acceptable to wear a dragon image and, in fact, that it is advisable to do so. By doing this, the dragon image takes on the energy of a talisman, bringing protection and luck.

Clashing imagery

- The clash of the dog and the dragon image – known as the clash of yang earth energy – causes a depression. So avoid placing a dog image in the dragon direction of Southeast 1 and a dragon image in the dog direction of Northwest 1.

- The clash of the rat and the horse indicates a clash of yang fire with yang water, and is a cause of mental disability. Avoid this by ensuring rat images are not in the South and horse images are not in the North.

- The clash of the ox with the sheep is a clash of yin earth. Here, the sheep must not be placed in the ox direction of Northeast 1, and the ox should not be placed in the sheep direction of Southwest 1.

- The clash of the tiger with the monkey indicates wood clashing with metal. Here, the energies are both yang so it is an active clash – any battles between these two are usually fought out in the open and are fierce. It is better that the tiger should not be in the Southwest 3 direction and that the monkey should not be in the Northeast 3 direction.

- The clash of the rabbit with the rooster is also wood clashing with metal, but here the energies are yin so any opposition between these two will be silent, covert, and underhand. It is absolutely vital that the rabbit must not be in the West and that the rooster must not be in the East. Otherwise, there will be aggravation for the animal sign afflicted by the presence of the enemy in its own home camp.

- The clash of the boar and the snake is a clash of fire with water, but this clash is a yin chi clash so animosities here are undercurrents. The hostility between the two will never break out into the open, so it is all the more dangerous. The clash here can cause problems with accidents related to water, so make certain that the boar is not placed in the Southeast 3 direction and the Snake is never placed in the Northwest 3 direction. In this case, the presence of a hidden enemy in your home direction will bring financial loss.

Watching out for astrological afflictions in the home 112

It is beneficial to use the astrological wheel (see Tip 110) to clear your home systematically of astrological afflictions. This means investigating the spaces that represent the personal astrology spaces of every single member of the family living there. Look out for physical afflictions, such as beams and sharp edges pointing to identified corners, and make a special effort to neutralize them. For example, if the patriarch of the family is a horse person then you must make sure that the South (which is the horse direction) is not hurt by anything sharp or pointed. The South should also not be locked up, nor should there be a toilet or a kitchen in the South as these press down on the horse person's good fortune.

Avoiding your enemies

In the same way, also ensure that the directions of all family members are not inadvertently made dangerous by having images of their astrological enemies placed in them. The remedy here is simply to place these symbols elsewhere.

Please do understand that astrological enemies are dangerous only when they are placed in the home direction of a resident. Placed anywhere else, and they are perfectly safe. As an example of this, although the rat and horse are enemies, as long as the horse image is not placed in the North (the Rat's direction), and

it is placed in its own direction of the South, the horse can bring enormous good fortune to the rat-born resident.

The Southwest 3 direction is the animal-sign direction of the Monkey. Don't place a Tiger in this location, as the Monkey and Tiger are astrological enemies. Place the Tiger in his natural sector, which is Northeast 3.

113 Carry images of your secret friend to invoke sincere friendship

An Ox person will benefit from wearing images of the rooster, snake, ox, and rat.

One of the easiest and most effective way of ensuring good personalized feng shui based on your astrology chart is simply to carry images of your allies and secret friends (see Tip 110). This is something known to the Chinese since forever, and it is the reason why there are always so many images of the 12 astrological animal signs.

The best way to wear them is on a charm bracelet. Each person should wear a minimum of three – although four are best – animal signs, made up of the three animals that represent your affinity animals as well as your secret friend.

Know your affinity animals and friends

1 **A dragon person** will benefit from wearing a charm bracelet with the monkey, rat, dragon, and rooster.

2 **A monkey person** will benefit from wearing a charm bracelet with the monkey, rat, dragon, and snake.

3 **A rat person** will benefit from wearing a charm bracelet with the monkey, rat, dragon, and ox.

4 **A snake person** will benefit from wearing a charm bracelet with the rooster, snake, ox, and monkey.

5 **A rooster person** will benefit from wearing a charm bracelet with the rooster, snake, ox, and dragon.

6 **An ox person** will benefit from wearing a charm bracelet with the rooster, snake, ox, and rat.

7 **A boar person** will benefit from wearing a charm bracelet with the boar, sheep, rabbit, and tiger.

8 **A sheep person** will benefit from wearing a charm bracelet with the boar, sheep, rabbit, and horse.

9 **A rabbit person** will benefit from wearing a charm bracelet with the boar, sheep, rabbit, and dog.

10 **A dog person** will benefit from wearing a charm bracelet with the dog, horse, tiger, and rabbit.

11 **A horse person** will benefit from wearing a charm bracelet with the dog, horse, tiger, and sheep.

12 **A tiger person** will benefit from wearing a charm bracelet with the dog, horse, tiger, and boar.

Charm bracelets displaying Chinese animals activate the protection of your astrological allies.

Strengthen the element of your animal sign 114

The final activity related to astrological feng shui is to take note of the element of your animal sign and to strengthen its home location by placing something of the producing element there. For example, the dragon, sheep, ox, and dog are described as having the earth element.

Animal elements

- The sheep and the ox are already residing in earth locations; the dragon, however, resides in a wood location, which makes it weak. It is a good idea to strengthen the dragon location of Southeast 1 with fire energy. This will enhance the chi essence of the dragon. The dog is located in the Northwest 1 location, which is metal. This exhausts the dog so the Northwest 1 dog direction should also be enhanced with fire energy.

- The rooster and monkey are both intrinsically metal. The rooster is in the West so it is strong enough and the monkey is in the Southwest, which makes it even stronger. For these two animal signs, there is no need to do anything more.

- The snake and the horse are both fire element. The horse is located in the South, whose element is also fire, so the horse is fine. But the snake is even better, because it is located in the Southeast, which is wood. So for these two animal signs, there is no need to do anything more.

- The tiger and the rabbit are both wood element. Note that the tiger is located in the Northeast, which is earth. Wood overcomes earth, but it is distracted. It is necessary to strengthen the tiger with water energy. So

You can bring the fire element into a room by introducing reds and oranges into the decor.

placing water here would benefit anyone who is born in the year of the tiger. The rabbit meanwhile is in the East, which is also wood, so the rabbit is fine. There is no need to do anything more.

- The rat and the pig – or boar – are both water element. The rat is in the North, which is also water, so there is no need to do anything more. The pig is in the Northwest 3 direction, which is metal, where it is being enhanced, so again there is no need to do anything.

In Chinese astrology, the boar, or pig's, associated element is water, and his compass direction is Northwest 3.

115 Keeping track of changes in annual and monthly chi energy

This aspect of feng shui practice is not fully understood by many practitioners. It is part of the flying star system, but the annual and monthly charts that reveal the constantly changing locations of affliction star numbers and auspicious star numbers are different from the flying star charts of houses. The annual and monthly charts must be read in conjunction with the charts of houses. So basically what we end up with is a combination of five numbers in each compass location – these numbers give us a pretty accurate picture of what the luck of houses looks like from month to month and from year to year. To recap, these numbers comprise:

1 The period number (in the house chart).

2 The water star number (in the house chart).

3 The mountain star number (in the house chart).

4 The annual star number (in the year chart).

5 The monthly star number (in the month chart).

You are already familiar with the house charts of both period 7 and period 8 (see Tips 37 and 38), so what you now need is to become familiar with how to obtain the year charts and the month charts to give you an up-to-date picture of how the chi energy is changing in your house. The meanings of the numbers do not change, so the affliction numbers remain 2, 5, 3, and 7, each with its individual type of misfortune. Likewise, the auspicious numbers are still 8, 9, 1, 6, and 4, each bringing its own type of good fortune.

116 Feng shui updates for each new year

At the start of each new year based on the Chinese Hsia calendar, which always begins on February 4 of each year, it is important to assess the new year chart and the monthly charts to familiarize yourself with the new energy of that year.

Here, we follow the Hsia calendar months, which are different from lunar months and the months of the Western calendar. The Hsia calendar is equivalent to the solar calendar the Chinese use to calculate

The Chinese almanac, or Tong Sing, bases its predictions on the Hsai calender.

the beginning of spring, and when to plant and when to harvest. It is the calendar on which many of the oracles and destiny methods contained in the Chinese Almanac, or Tong Sing (see left) are based.

Once you understand the importance of these charts you will be able to use them to update the feng shui of your home. Bear in mind that it is the year and month afflictions that bring you the aggravations of daily living (see the sample charts opposite in Tip 117) such as feeling exhausted, quarrelling with people for no apparent reason, suddenly falling ill, getting robbed, being hit with an unexpected disaster, and just about everything going wrong. When this happens you can suspect it is the year and month stars playing havoc with your life, especially if you know that the rest of your space feng shui is fine.

Be alert to dangerous star afflictions each year and every month 117

You must be absolutely alert to the dangerous star number afflictions that show up in the year and month charts. What are you looking for? Basically, you want to look out for:

- The misfortune star 5
- The illness star 2
- The quarrelsome star 3
- The violent star 7

Look at which compass sector they are located at in the year chart.

Forewarned is forearmed

Having found the location of these troublesome star numbers, see which part of your house is affected. If, for example, it is your facing palace (the part of your house that is in front and that probably has the main door) then you need to be extra careful. This is because everyone passes through that part of the house and if it is afflicted by the number 2 star, residents are sure to

SE	S	SW
2 Illness	**7** Burglary	**9** Lucky
1 Lucky	**3** 2006 Fire dog	**5** FIVE Yellow
6 Lucky	Auspicious **8** 3 Killings	Gr Duke **4** ♥Peach♥ Blossom
NE	N	NW

E (left) ... W (right)

This annual chart for 2006 shows the location of lucky and unlucky numbers. If the placement of unlucky numbers coincides with those on a monthly chart, bad luck can intensify so you will need to be vigilant in using feng shui cures. For annual charts, go to www.wofs.com; see also page 160.

Always identify any troublesome stars that afflict your main door, as this affects the luck of the whole house, rather than just the area around the main entrance itself.

fall ill. Worse, if the month 2 is also there and if the mountain or water star is also a 2, then the accumulation of 2s will bring powerful misfortune energy to the residents.

Then it will definitely be necessary to put cures into place or, better still, residents should consider taking a vacation during the month when the 2s congregate like this. This same outcome will also occur when the 2s congregate in the dining room area or in the bedroom.

If the year 2 is joined by the month 3, then illness leads to quarrels and severe consequences. The important part of the investigation is to determine if the bad star numbers affect any of the important parts of your house. Needless to say, if the affliction numbers fall inside a kitchen, storeroom, or toilet, you have no cause for worry.

118   "5 yellow" afflictions cause feng shui havoc

Of all the affliction star numbers, it is the number 5, known as the 5 yellow, that everyone should be most sensitive to (see also Tips 49 and 50). This is because the 5 is a very powerful earth star, which brings a whole range of woes, from financial loss to unexpected obstacles, and from the sudden onset of severe danger to great aggravation, worry, and misfortune. The 5 is the ultimate disaster star number and everyone succumbs to its influence. Its severity depends upon whether there are more than three 5s in the same grid or sector of the home. For example, if the mountain star is 5, the annual star is 5, and the month star is 5, all occurring in the same sector, then residents with their main door located in the afflicted sector must remedy the situation using strong metal energy.

The worst case is when star number afflictions of this type occur in the sector containing the main door, as this brings misfortune influences to everyone in the house. If it occurs in a bedroom, then only those in that room are afflicted. Some feng shui practitioners have found that the 5 yellow is so powerful that it is a good idea to move out of the room during the time it is under its influence.

How to overcome the 5 yellow

To overcome the 5 yellow, the best cure is to use metal energy literally to exhaust the earth energy of the number. Thus, using all-metal windchimes is an excellent antidote, as the chimes also gives off the sound of metal. In period 7, using a six-rod windchime made of brass would be a great cure. In this present period, however, which is period 8, using a five-element pagoda made of brass is considered to be more powerful still. This is because period 8 is an earth period when the 5 yellow becomes even stronger. The five-element pagoda is a traditional and classical cure (see left). Try to obtain a pagoda with the powerful Chien metal trigram stamped on its base.

Using the pagoda

The best way to use the five-element pagoda cure is to unscrew each of the element shapes that make up the charm and fill it to the brim with earth taken from your garden. Then seal the earth inside the pagoda. This will symbolically lock up the 5 yellow, rendering it harmless.

A five-element pagoda exhausts the negative energy of the 5 yellow affliction. If your home is large, you might need to use more than one.

An afflicted main door is much worse than a afflicted room, because the main door dictates the good fortune or misfortune of the whole property. If your main door is affected by the 5 yellow, display a five-element pagoda (right) in the foyer or hall.

Neutralize the number 2 illness star 119

The illness star 2 is also an earth star, and when it flies into your bedroom it increases the chances of illness. When more than three number 2 flying stars occur in a particular sector, illness chi becomes extremely strong indeed, and residents will need to be particularly careful to avoid succumbing to a serious ailment.

When the illness star 2 occupies your bedroom, hang a windchime there to protect against possible illness until the star's negative influence has passed.

Take precautions

The best way to overcome the illness star is to use the metal energies of the brass windchime, preferably one that has six hollow rods and also a wu lou image somewhere on the chime itself. The number 6 stands for big metal, while the rods should be hollow to allow the chi to move within it. Hang the windchimes in the sector where the 2 stars are accumulating, but be careful not to hang them so high that they are over someone's head – this is deemed to be potentially harmful. The chimes should ideally be hung at about waist level against a wall.

Hang windchimes halfway up a wall. The best anti illness windchime has six hollow rods, a Pa Kua coin and a small wu lou (see Tip 46). Another excellent cure is a wu lou with an image of the Eight Immortals.

120 Watch out for the Grand Duke Jupiter creating problems

Every year it is very important to find out where the god of the year, also known as the Grand Duke Jupiter, or Tai Sui in Chinese, is located. This is not as difficult as it sounds because in each year he occupies the 15° of space that corresponds to the animal sign of the year. For example, in the year of the rooster, 2005, the Tai Sui was in the West. And in the year 2006, the year of the dog, he is in the 15° corresponding to the Northwest 1 direction. If you refer to the astrology wheel (see Tip 108) you will be able to locate the Tai Sui with no difficulty from year to year.

A Chinese coin displaying images of Pi Kan can easily be placed anywhere in a home to guard against the Grand Duke Jupiter.

How to deal with the Grand Duke

From a feng shui perspective, there are some basic rules regarding the Tai Sui.

1 Never sit facing the direction that has the Tai Sui in any year, even when that direction is your best direction based on the Kua formula. Confronting the Tai Sui this way leads to misfortunes and problems. So note that in 2005 you should not sit facing West and Northwest 1.

2 Never undertake any type of digging, banging, or cutting in the location occupied by the Tai Sui. To ignore this rule is to invite problems and worry into your household.

A Pi Yao figurine (above right) or a pair of Pi Kan dragon dogs (below) protects against Tai Su, or the Grand Duke Jupiter.

3 Always place a Pi Yao or a pair of Pi Kan or Pi Xie in the direction where the Tai Sui is located. This is really a simple way to appease the Tai Sui, thereby ensuring his support. Another way to do this is to sit with the Tai Sui's direction behind you. This ensures that you will enjoy victory in all your endeavors.

4 Finally, note that if yours is the animal sign that corresponds to the animal directly opposite the Tai Sui, then you should take extra care that year. You should have the Pi Yao or a pair of Pi Xie or Pi Kan to assist you. Thus, for example, in the year of the rooster 2005, everyone born in the year of the rabbit should take note of this advice. And in 2006, the year of the dog, the advice applies to all those born in the year of the dragon.

Avoid coming under the influence of the "3 killings" 121

This is a well-known annual chi affliction called in Chinese the *Sarm sart,* which literally translates as "3 killings." The theory is that whoever is residing in the part of the house that the 3 killings flies to will endure three types of misfortunes, mainly related to loss – loss of your good name, loss of love and/or friendship, and loss of money. The 3 killings is an affliction that affects only the four cardinal directions – North, East, South, and West – and it changes location in your home from year to year.

Locating the 3 killings

To find out where the 3 killings will be in each year, just take note of which animal sign is ruling in that year. Thus:

ANIMAL	Year	DIRECTION OCCUPIED BY THE 3 KILLINGS
Rooster	2005	East
Ox	2009	East
Snake	2013	East
Boar	2007	West
Rabbit	2011	West
Sheep	2015	West
Rat	2008	South
Dragon	2012	South
Monkey	2016	South
Dog	2006, 2018	North
Tiger	2010	North
Horse	2014	North

122 Dragon horses remedy the 3 killings

- When the 3 killings is in the West, place open yang water – in other words, moving water – in that sector.

- When it is in the South, the cure for the 3 killings is made stronger by the presence of crystals.

- When it is in the North, place a strong and sturdy plant there too.

Unlike the Tai Sui, or Grand Duke Jupiter, whose direction must never be confronted, the direction of the 3 killings must be confronted. You should never turn your back to the 3 killings –

Check out your sitting direction at dinner and while you are working to avoid the 3 killings.

The best general remedy against the 3 killings is to place three chi lin, or dragon horses, wherever it occurs in your home. Also, note the following:

- When it is in the East, shine a bright light in the corner there.

for if you do, you are sure to experience some type of misfortune. In 2006, when the 3 killings flies to the North, you should make sure that the North is not behind you when you sit or give a speech, even if North is your best direction according to the Kua formula.

Chi lin, or dragon horses, are the best protection against the danger of the 3 killings, which brings three kinds of bad luck – loss of wealth, loss of health, and loss of relationships.

Be wary of the number 7 star – especially when annual and monthly

123

You need to buy or create a running water feature to exhaust the bad energy wherever the water star 7 falls in your home. Display a ready-made indoor water fountain (left) – the Laughing Buddhas set around it also activate for prosperity – or make your own feature by using a small water pump placed in a bowl of polished pebbles or crystals.

Now that we are in period 8, the number 7 star has turned nasty, having reverted back to its original violent nature. The number 7 star is also regarded as the burglary star, which causes residents affected by it to be robbed, often with associated violence. The number 7 star is officially known as the broken soldier red star. The best way to overcome it is with running water. This is the element that will exhaust the number 7 star, rendering it less potent.

You should be especially wary of the number 7 star when it occurs as a yearly and monthly star. Also take note that many of the period 7 flying star charts have the double 7 water and mountain stars – and in this new period they must be remedied by the inclusion of water in the afflicted sector of your home. Better still is to change the house from a period 7 into a period 8 house (see Tip 39).

Q & A

Q: *What is the simplest water remedy to use to protect my home from burglary?*

A: To counter the burglary star with water chi, you need the presence of physical water – a picture of water will not do. Only when you have yang water present is it strong enough to exhaust the burglary star. An excellent way to achieve this is to buy the type of small water feature that has an integral pump to circulate the water.

124   Red cushions or a red painting for the number 3 star

If you do not want to invest in red cushions or re-paint a room, display an inexpensive, simple red wall hanging with complementary accessories in order to "burn out" the quarrelsome number 3 star.

The hostility and severity of the number 3 quarrelsome star is regarded with suspicion by many feng shui practitioners as being a particularly fearsome star number. It brings hostility and misunderstanding into your midst and it is the star most associated with relationship problems between loved ones. The number 3 star causes misunderstandings, fights, and court cases to arise as if from nowhere. It is a very dangerous star, as it can also cause heartbreak and depression.

Fire energy

The way to overcome the number 3 star – especially when it occurs as the year and month star as well as the mountain or water star – is to use fire energy. Use bright lights, use lots of bright red energy on cushion covers, as table napkins, as carpet and curtains, or even use red as the dominant color in artworks. I once recommended to a friend that she paint an entire wall red in a bid to get rid of a particularly troublesome court case that was facing her husband. He was powerless to do anything legally to affect the outcome of the case, but once the wall was painted red, it was surprisingly dropped. He has, since that time, become an ardent feng shui fan.

A cure to overcome the hostile number 3 star is this triangular, red-colored crystal, which manifests perfect fire chi to overcome ill-fortune.

PROJECT
Using element shapes

Each of the five Chinese elements – water, fire, earth, wood, and metal – has an associated shape. The shape for the fire element is the triangle, so any decorative item that bears this shape and is red reinforces the element energy. Look for the triangle in borders on throws, cushion trims, within paintings and collages, lampshades, and lamp base designs, and other home furnishings.

Watch that your renovations do not activate affliction stars 125

One of the easiest ways to maintain good feng shui is to "renovate" your home regularly. This need not be a major undertaking, but it is still an excellent way to ensure that chi energy never becomes stagnant or sour by keeping it constantly moving and energized. Sometimes just moving the furniture out of its regular place and moving it back again is enough, as it forces the chi energy to be disturbed and is thus activated.

Annual rotation

Renovations can be a series of annual jobs that keep the house well maintained. I always renovate my home moving from sector to sector – repainting, changing a door or window, and so forth. But I always make sure to keep tabs on three of the afflictions of any year:

1 The Grand Duke Jupiter, or Tai Sui.

2 The three killings, or sam sart.

3 The five yellow.

I take note of where the Grand Duke, three killings or five yellow reside each year and I make very certain that those locations are never disturbed by any of the renovations. Even if I ever have to renovate a major portion of my home, I make certain that I never start or end the work in any of the locations occupied by these three afflictions.

Plan maintenance work to avoid beginning or ending in any afflicted sector.

Look for the very special 8 star 126

The annual flying star feng shui chart does not just have affliction star numbers. This chart also reveals the most lucky location in the home for the year. This will, of course, be where the number 8 star flies to in any year. In this current period, the number 8 star is a powerfully auspicious star number. In 2006 the lucky star 8 flies to the North, and this brings great good fortune to those living in houses that either sit in the North direction (facing South) or which sit South (facing North). North belongs to the water element, and the creature of the North is the Tortoise. Remember that the number 8 is also the strongest in terms of chi energy, so do activate this sector to experience the best of its auspicious chi essence.

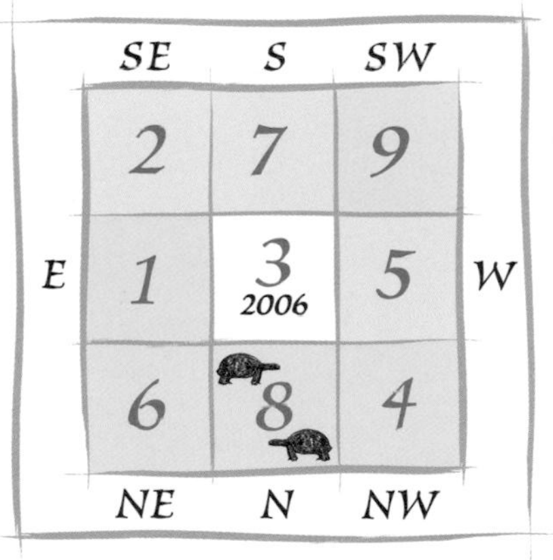
SE
S
SW
2
7
9
E
1
3
2006
5
W
6
8
4
NE
N
NW

Activate the lucky 8 sector in your home with the auspicious animal of the North, the tortoise. Displaying two cranes entwined on a tortoise will bring additional career luck.

127 Number 6 brings heaven chi – in the current period it has renewed vitality

The number 6 is the symbol of heaven and also of the Chien trigram, which is the strongest yang trigram. It also enjoys renewed vigor in period 8, so wherever the 6 occurs in the annual chart it brings the luck of heaven. In 2006, the number 6 flies to the Northeast, where it becomes even stronger. To energize it then, invest in six crystal balls or six wish-fulfilling jewels.

The number 6 is regarded as one of the three auspicious white numbers, the other two being 1 and 8. Whenever these three numbers occur together in any combination, they spell incredible good fortune for everyone. Thus, vehicle number plates with 168 or telephone numbers that end with 168 are especially auspicious and much favored by the Chinese.

In 2006, the number 6 flies into the sector of the compass occupied by the Tiger.

Six crystal balls placed in the Northwest sector of the home brings in heaven chi.

Number 4 brings romance luck   128

The number 4 is a much-misunderstood number. To many, the word 4 in Chinese sounds like "death," and therefore as such it has never been a very popular number with the Chinese. However, to those who know flying star feng shui, the number 4 brings peach blossom luck. This means love, the type of love that has a good chance of leading to commitment and marriage.

Look out for the number 4 in your flying star chart to identify the romance sectors of your home for that year. The good fortune romance sector in annual flying star charts changes from year to year

Two fours in the bedroom

The number 4 is similarly welcome in a flying star chart, preferably when it appears as a mountain star (to the left of a large period number). When the 4s occur together in the sector of your home where your bedroom is located, it signifies marriage luck. But when there is an excess of water energy – whether because of the presence of physical water or the intangible energy of the number 1 water star – the love luck turns insidious and negative. The number 4 combined with 1 or 4 with water often lead to sexual scandals and messy infidelity.

^{6}2^8	$^{}$④^1	^{8}9^6
^{2}6^3	^{1}7^4	^{9}8^5
^{3}5^2	^{7}1^7	^{5}3^9

The 4/1 combination helps writers   129

The 4/1 star combination in a flying star chart brings literary luck as well as romance and marriage, and it favors those for whom writing is their profession.

Book authors and other writers living or working in rooms favored by the number 4 and the number 1 as the mountain and water star (to the left and right of a period number respectively) will enjoy special benefits. The way to activate this auspicious star is by placing healthy, vibrant plants in the location of the 4/1.

Use healthy plants to activate creativity luck for writers.

Part Three

Safeguarding the Home

OVERCOMING BAD LUCK FROM THE TEN DIRECTIONS

As you delve deeper into feng shui, it becomes increasingly apparent how important it is to be totally familiar with the various orientations of your home. This is because so many of the different formulas and methods of feng shui are directly associated with compass directions. The amateur practitioner basically works with the eight compass directions, while those who go deeper into analyzing the flying star charts of their homes (see Tip 30) expand these eight directions into 24 by dividing each main direction into three sub-directions. We refer to these 24 sub-directions as the 24 mountains of feng shui. In addition to the eight main directions, however, feng shui also identifies an additional two directions from which both good and bad luck can originate – from the top (for example, the sky or heaven energy) and from the bottom (for example, from the earth).

In feng shui there are different symbols that spell protection for the home, and the Chinese are especially fond of the celestial guardians – the dragon, the tiger, phoenix, and tortoise. In larger buildings frequented by many people, such as temples and palaces, favored guardians are the massive lions or Fu dogs – many different kinds can be seen in the Forbidden City in Beijing. In other parts of China, the dragons Pi Yao or Pi Xie are popular. In modern feng shui practice, we can also safeguard our homes by cleverly applying the exhaustive, or controlling, cycle of the five elements – see page 9.

Bad luck can come from the 10 directions 130

To safeguard your home or office it is important to see if it is being afflicted with bad luck from the eight major directions of North, South, East, West, Southwest, Northwest, Northeast, and Southeast, as well as from the top and bottom. Each of these directions can carry with it an ill-wind or afflicted chi energy capable of bringing different types of bad luck. At its worst, such bad luck can cause loss of life, fatal accidents, and other tragic developments, so it is a good idea to develop what I refer to as the "feng shui eye". This means that your subconscious will immediately alert you to anything negative that is perhaps the result of some new structure or development in your immediate environment.

Cures and remedies

By being alert in this way and by becoming familiar with ways of deflecting such bad luck, you will take your practice of feng shui to a new level of effectiveness. Take note, however, that when it comes to the compass directions, bad luck is best dealt with using cures based on the exhaustive cycle of the five elements (see page 9). The idea is to exhaust the bad luck chi energy that is coming at your house. The direction from which the bad luck originates will enable you to devise the cure that will most effectively curtail its strength. Cures and remedies will work as long as you apply the cycle of the five elements correctly, and the good news is that you can be as creative as you wish in using this principle.

Do not allow talk of so-called "classical feng shui" or "ancient feng shui" to confuse you. The important thing is to understand the basic premise of feng shui cures and then apply your creativity and rational mind to set up the necessary antidotes to whatever is sending you the bad luck. For bad luck from above and below, however, the remedies are based on the theory of yin and yang energy, as you will see in the following tips.

The ten directions bring good and bad energy. The facing direction of your home, and the direction you face when you sit and sleep, will therefore tap positive or negative types of luck.

Directions and elements

DIRECTION	ELEMENT
North	Water
South	Fire
East	Wood
West	Metal
Southwest	Earth
Northwest	Metal
Northeast	Earth
Southeast	Wood

131   Overcome bad luck from above with pure incense energy

If you feel that the air above you is sending the bad energy, perhaps because the air is polluted, or you live in an area affected by smog, shining a bright light upward goes a long way to neutralizing the invisible chi pressing down on you. Another excellent way of dealing with bad energy from the heavens is to use pure incense energy. The best incense to use is made from high mountain herbs growing in places where the environment is clean and pure. You can perform a weekly incense ritual by burning it every Friday evening at around 6pm.

Bad vibes cured by incense

Incense energy is incredibly powerful in cleansing the negative vibes that are inadvertently brought into the house. I recall once when old friends came to spend a weekend with us and it turned into a horrible time. For some reason the two of them got off to a bad start and were becoming surprisingly nasty to each other. Before I knew what was happening, we had a full-blown quarrel on our hands. They were practically at each other's throats, and by the end of the Saturday evening, the air was thick with tension. Old aggravations surfaced, and what should have been a lovely evening, reminiscing about good times, turned ugly. We got up from the dining table and moved to the living room, but that just seemed to make things worse.

On Sunday morning we sent our friends off to the airport to catch their flight home to Hong Kong, but when we got back to the house another quarrel flared up between us over something so trivial I cannot now even recall what it was. Anger hung in the air. At this point, I decided to burn my special mountain incense, which comes from the high peaks of the Himalayas where the air is so clean, crisp, and pure. Incense from such a place has magical powers of purification. I took a bath before performing the incense purification ritual as I needed time to cool down.

When I felt sufficiently composed, I walked with my incense clockwise around my dining and living rooms, each time letting the incense rise and mingle. By the evening, the atmosphere had returned to normal. Later, I sent some of this incense to my friend after she called to apologize but also to inform me that the differences between her and her husband seemed to have escalated. I taught her to perform the same ritual in all the rooms of their home, just as I had done, and the following week I was rewarded with a happy phone call from my friend telling me that the two of them had made up.

Keep bad luck from the earth by surrounding your home with plants 132

If you are living in an area that is known to have been used for "bad purposes," such as a burial ground or an execution ground in the past, it is possible that the earth energy of the area will retain lingering traces of death-like yin energy. Such places are subjected to what in feng shui is termed "yin spirit formation," which is similar to that caused by flying star numbers (see Tip 30), except that here the chi energy is caused by something tangible.

Overcoming tragic chi

The earth on which our houses are built always carries chi energy – which can be good or bad.

It will be bad, however, when there are traces of unhappiness, or tragic chi. The best way to overcome this is to surround yourself with growth energy. Plants, trees, and shrubs are the best antidote as they all give off precious yang energy. As plants grow they send out pure, living energy. Scientists have confirmed this by telling us, for example, that trees and plants produce oxygen as they grow. In the same way, the roots of trees and plants represent the best way of sending yang energy into the ground around us, thereby reducing the influence of yin stagnation.

Round-leaved plants, such as a money plant, are auspicious in feng shui.

Having plants, shrubs, and trees close to your home encourages the flow of positive yang energy. Decorating your outside spaces and trees with attracting lighting (above) also brings in growth energy.

133 The grounding cord ritual to protect against bad earth energy

It is also possible to use the visualization method to counter bad energy arising from the earth. It has already been acknowledged that the human consciousness and the human mind are potentially the greatest sources of positive yang chi. So those of you who are adept at using meditation techniques to practice inner feng shui on your home have a head start.

Stabilize your mind before you start – remember, you should be feeling calm, strong, and relaxed at all times as you work through the meditation outlined below.

Grounding meditation

Before you do anything, go out into the garden and breathe in the fresh air. It is always better to do this in bright sunshine. Then go back indoors.

1 Sit with your spine straight and eyes gently cast downward, and set your motivation. This should always be to the benefit of others rather than yourself. In this case, let your motivation be to create a calm and happy home for your family.

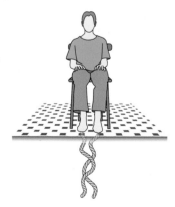

2 Breathe normally and let your breath get deeper and deeper. Let your thoughts settle and prepare yourself to create visualizations inside your mind.

3 When you are ready, visualize your body sending a firm grounding cord into the earth under your home. Let the cord go down deep and then picture your body sending light into the cord, which is lit up. It is also sending rays of bright sunlight into the earth around it.

4 Try and hold this picture for a few minutes before gently bringing the cord back up again. Rest a while before getting up.

When you are ready, go back out into the sunshine and take several deep breaths to replenish your own chi energy.

From the compass directions use the five elements to cure bad energy   134

Bad energy can take the form of hostile structures, large ugly buildings, a new elevated road, or anything that you instinctively feel is threatening (see also Tips 1 and 5). If you notice something like this, the best thing to do is check the orientation of the offending structure so that you can determine the direction the bad energy is coming from. Take directions using a compass when standing at the front of your house. Once you have this information, follow these guidelines:

Use a compass to accurately determine the direction bad energy hits your home. Hostile chi emanates from external structures such as pylons and the edges of nearby buildings.

- When bad energy attacks from the Northwest or West, use fire or water energy. Fire energy will destroy the bad energy while water energy will exhaust it. How strong you want your cure to be depends on how large the threatening structure is. Fire energy is a bright light, while water energy comes in the form of a water feature, such as a fountain.

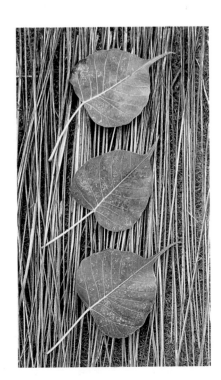

The Bodhi tree guards against bad energy coming into the North of your home. Bodhi leaves (see right) are thought to protect you from the evil eye. If you are lucky enough to have a Bodhi tree you can also use it to enhance your luck – plant it in the East, Southeast, or South sector of your garden for this purpose.

- Overcome bad luck from the South with earth energy by placing crystals in this direction. The crystals will exhaust the bad luck chi.

- When misfortune strikes from the North, get a cactus plant or a Bodhi tree (also known as the tree of wisdom), which has a thorny trunk and leaves that, although beautiful, can be dangerous if they come into contact with your eyes. The leaf from the Bodhi tree is said to be excellent for overcoming the evil eye – in other words, negative energy coming from people who may be jealous of you.

- Bad energy from the East and Southeast can be overcome using fire energy from a bright light. So for bad things emanating from these compass points, shine a powerful spotlight in that direction.

- Overcome bad luck from the Southwest using metal windchime energy. The sound of metal is excellent for this affliction.

- Control bad chi from the Northeast with metal chi, such as bells and windchimes.

135 Get rich and happy with the Laughing Buddha

The Chinese are especially fond of the laughing Buddha (see him in Tip 156). Indeed, there are few Chinese homes that do not have at least one figurine of this broadly smiling, fat-bellied icon of prosperity and happiness.

The Buddha as remedy for the 3 star

Inviting his image into the home not only brings wealth and prosperity, it also means that everyone living there will be happy and in a perpetual good mood. With his infectious, happy, smiling face, it is impossible to be otherwise. If you can find a Laughing Buddha dressed in bright red garments it is also the perfect cure for the quarrelsome star 3 of the flying star system. This is because red represents fire energy, which exhausts the negative energy of the 3 star.

However, I always advise my students and clients to have a Laughing Buddha anyway – whether or not the quarrelsome star afflicts them. His presence in the home can do no harm, and can only do good.

136 Restoring yin and yang balance in the tai chi of your home

The theory of yin and yang applies to proportion, color, and shape in a designated space.

The yin yang symbol.

Many people forget this most basic of feng shui practices – creating balance in every room of the home as well as in the whole house. The "tai chi" is the term used to describe the yin yang symbol, and according to the guidelines on practical applications, every designated space should be regarded as a tai chi. Thus, the tai chi of space can be a large, sumptuous mansion or a humble, two-roomed house; it can be the whole house or it can be a single room; it can even be just your desk. It depends on what you consider to be your circle of space. Once you designate your space, an important thing to do is look at the objects that fill it. Then ask yourself if there is a balance of yin and yang there. In other words, is the space too bright or too dark? Are there too many plants, or is the space too stagnant? Or is your desk crowded with yang symbols?

Balancing yin and yang means there should be a healthy mix of each – though it is great to have a little more yang than yin. So temper bright colors with some shadier neutrals and add some dark colors as well. The balance of yin and yang ensures a healthy combination of these complementary forces.

Dragon and phoenix vases for peace and harmony 137

I nvest in a golden dragon or phoenix vase, as this is regarded as one of the most satisfying ways to create a calm, happy, and prosperous home. For centuries, Chinese royalty and wealthy mandarins alike lavishly decorated their palaces and homes with vases. There would not be a single room that did not have pairs of vases created from porcelain and cloisonné, and decorated with different types of auspicious symbols.

In the outer, more public rooms, gigantic vases decorated in brilliant hues and featuring various longevity and prosperity symbols would be used to flank entrances and doorways, while deeper into the inner quarters of the home, vases made of gold, cloisonné, and special porcelain would be used to highlight important corners.

Wealth vases

In yet more private inner sanctums, families would have at least one wealth vase. This would be passed down from generation to generation and its presence in the home would ensure the steady accumulation of wealth within the family. Wealth vases are filled and consecrated with special substances that symbolize family assets and wealth, such as real gold, diamonds, and other precious stones. In addition, wealth vases would also contain soil from the property of a wealthy person and, if possible, cash from a wealthy person, in the form of a few coins. Symbolically, this effectively borrows his or her wealth chi and activates the wealth vase.

Vases are considered to be one of the eight precious objects in Chinese Buddhism, although as a symbolic presence in the home its popularity goes beyond the boundaries of religious or spiritual significance. In Chinese the word "vase" is ping, which also sounds like "peace."

Vases this shape and color – ox-blood red – are excellent feng shui. The golden dragon and phoenix image symbolize a happy marriage blessed with prosperity.

The image of the phoenix always symbolizes wonderful opportunities coming your way. By itself, the phoenix is a powerful symbol, attracting a sudden surge of good fortune. The phoenix is also the king of the birds, and bird energy always brings good news.

138 A rosewood Ru Yi strengthens the breadwinner's chi

In the old days, men of power and authority in China carried a scepter called the Ru Yi – often made of jade, carved with auspicious objects or fashioned in gold, and studded with precious gemstones. Even the emperor carried this symbol of imperial authority and royal power – said effectively to transmit the authority and power of his lifeforce. Since then, the Ru Yi has been revered as a symbol of high authority.

Today, placing the Ru Yi in your home and office is believed to confer the chi of leadership and influence. If you are a manager, or work in a supervisory capacity, the Ru Yi will ensure that your authority is acknowledged and that your judgments are respected. It is the best feng shui tool for managers and executives. Placed in the home, it is an amazingly effective tool for the breadwinner.

Ru Yi etiquette

It is, however, important to ensure that you get a Ru Yi that is in keeping with your status . . . so never place a Ru Yi in your home or office

A hand-carved rosewood Ru Yi is excellent for someone who is climbing the corporate career ladder. Rosewood is an auspicious wood in feng shui, and wood also symbolizes growth chi,

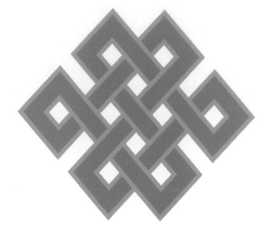

The mystic knot is a good fortune symbol often found on the Ru Yi.

that is plastic, or display one that is made of some cheap metal. You simply must look for a Ru Yi that suggests some real substance. The size is not as important as the way the Ru Yi has been crafted.

Remember that the Ru Yi represents the power of the high official who has the authority to make important decisions. So you need a Ru Yi that symbolizes this power. Only then will it confer powerful authority luck for those who want this type of influence.

When the Ru Yi is also embellished with other symbols of good fortune, such as the mystical knot or the 8 Immortals – manifesting eight types of good fortune associated with longevity, good health, happiness, success, and prosperity – it has added significance. Each of the Immortals signifies the attainment of the highest levels of success in different professions. Place the Ru Yi in your study at home in the Northwest direction.

Strengthen the mother by keeping the Southwest brightly lit 139

It is important that the Southwest corner of a home should not be missing – this is an affliction that can occur when you have an L-shaped house. If that corner is the Southwest, the chi it creates is that of a mother being away from the home more than normal. For example, it could be that she works lots of overtime or that she leaves the family.

The Southwest corner of every home should be kept clean and free of clutter and be decorated with auspicious symbols that benefit the earth chi of the mother. Hence, crystals or objects made of crystal would be excellent for enhancing this corner of the home. Also, keep the Southwest well lit at all times. Fire chi here strengthens the matriarchal energy. The benefits of observing these practices will be harmony and a flowering of love energy. The Southwest is, after all, also the universal corner for love and romance.

Wherever the Southwest sector is in your home, always kept it clean and well lit.

The Southwest's element is earth, symbolized by crystal. Place a crystal in this area of your home to encourage maternal presence.

Q & A

Q: *Which are the best crystals to use for strengthening the energy of the mother in the Southwest?*

A: When you use crystals in feng shui, it is always a good idea to invest in natural quartz, as this type of crystal has the best conductive energy. Buy a crystal cluster if you can find one that you like. If you find crystals too expensive, invest in a good-looking stone or boulder – these are often just as effective. Around 12 in (30 cm) across would do very nicely.

140   Use wall mirrors to double the good chi

If you have a separate dining room or dining area in a living room, hang a wall mirror to reflect the food on the table, which symbolizes abundance and wealth for the family. Don't use this method if you eat in your kitchen, as reflecting food preparation is seen as inauspicious.

Keep mirrors clean and shining to maximize their wealth-bringing chi.

You can use wall mirrors in your living or dining room to expand the size of these auspicious areas of your home. A large wall mirror in the dining room really does double the food placed on the dining table. This is excellent feng shui, as it means that the family will expand its wealth. To the Chinese, food always symbolizes prosperity, so doubling food on the table is symbolically an auspicious scenario.

Family occasions

It is vital that during important family occasions, when all members of the family gather for reunion dinners – New Year's Eve for the Chinese, Thanksgiving for Americans, Christmas day for Christians, and so forth – that the wall mirror captures and stores all the happiness chi that is created. This is excellent for ensuring that the home stays happy and that the family stays together. Please do note, however, that having mirrors in the dining room is completely different from having them in the kitchen. In fact, mirrors in the kitchen are a very risky proposition indeed. When you double the food being cooked, rather than doubling the food being eaten, it is symbolically inauspicious.

Wise ways with wish-fulfilling jewels for a dream come true 141

A very clever (and successful) way of attracting excellent opportunities is to surround an image of your animal sign with eight wish-fulfilling jewels. These are crystals fashioned into the shape of diamonds and other gemstones to simulate wish-fulfilling jewels, and they can be in different sizes and of various colors. So, if you are a person born in the Horse year, then this is your Chinese astrology sign, and you should place an image of a horse in the center of your eight gems.

You will find that many opportunities and good things start to come your way. Place this arrangement on your desk or in a part of your living room where it can be displayed to advantage. Since I am great believer in jewels, I place masses of these crystal gems in various

parts of my home and on my desk. I use mine as offerings to the Buddhas at my altar. Each jewel signifies a wish of mine. Since my wish list is very long you can imagine how many jewels I use.

You can also use wish-fulfilling jewels as altar offerings. The Chinese believe that this manifests your prayers into reality.

Create a spring in your home 142

Knowing the feng shui formulas and theories is one thing, putting that knowledge to work in a powerful and practical way is something else again. Over the years I have experimented with many water features to jumpstart my money luck. All of them worked pretty well – if you locate your water in the correct corners and then update them regularly in accordance with the changing chi energy of each year. But some methods really do work better than others.

Water chi

A very effective way with water is to create a natural spring in your home – or, at least, what looks like a natural spring. Select an auspicious corner inside your home and then dig a small circular hole about 18 in

(45 cm) in diameter – and certainly no larger than this. Install a pipe and then pump water through it so that it appears to sprout from the ground in a natural fashion. This is extremely auspicious in this current period of 8 – like the earth bringing you wealth in the form of water spouting from the ground.

Design your drainage system so the water is constantly recycled. And observe the annual taboos about digging and cutting in the corners where the annual afflictions are located – for example, the Grand Duke, the three killings, and the 5 yellow. Also note that it is inauspicious to dig a hole inside your home if you are resident there during any renovation work that is being carried out. In this case, you may have to locate your spring outside in the garden

143 Bring in the happy energy of a hundred birds

Displaying the phoenix, and images of lots of birds, helps send our prayers and wishes to heaven.

The hugely auspicious chi that is symbolized by birds is one of the most closely guarded secrets of the Taoist masters. These feathered creatures are incredibly efficient at sending our wishes and aspirations into the cosmos beyond. Birds are said to be the messengers of the gods, manifesting the powerful energy of the winds, and when you display beautiful decorative bird images or paintings of birds they symbolize harmony, romance, and loving relationships

The Taoists strongly approve of hundred birds paintings being displayed in the home as these bring all the different types of auspicious birds together – including the king of birds, the creature that brings everything auspicious – the phoenix. In the year of the bird (2005), bird energy is even more auspicious. And if you want to go all the way, I suggest you look for a painting or a photograph showing a million birds!

Note that:

- Mandarin ducks, swans, and geese signify romance and everlasting love

- Cranes symbolize longevity

- The rooster signifies triumph over gossip and competitive pressures

- Magpies bring good news

Q & A

Q: *Are there any birds that I should avoid?*

A: No – all birds have some beneficial meanings. So the eagle is a bird of protection, while the crow is a bird that brings messages from the heavens. Having said this, it is of course a good idea to invite in those birds that appeal to you, rather than bring in ones you do not like. When using good fortune or protective symbols, the main thing to bear in mind is that you and all members of your family should feel comfortable living with them. For example, I have two gigantic phoenixes made of brass flanking my doorway. My family love them, but some people might find them over the top. When using symbols, always take note of personal preferences.

Display the rooster at work to counteract disruptive office politics.

Calming symbols that smooth out sibling rivalry 144

If you have a very large family with many growing children living together, then it is a good idea to introduce calming energy into the home. For this task, all you need are smooth crystal balls or any other spheres, such as glass spheres. It is important that they should be smooth and are made of the type of semi-precious stones and quartz traditionally associated with emitting calming vibrations. The best of these are, of course, those spheres made of natural quartz crystal, placed in a cluster of six. The spheres can be of any size you wish.

The number 6 in this context is significant, since it is the number of calming heaven energy. If the natural quartz balls are beyond your budget, look for glass spheres made in different colors and shades of blue, green, lavender, and yellow. Place these on a coffee table or on shelves in full view of everyone going in and out of the house. In time, you will come to appreciate the calming influence of these wonderful spheres. They are especially good for dissolving all thoughts of rivalry and competition between siblings, and even between spouses.

Glass or crystal spheres promote better relationships between siblings – display six together to symbolize calm.

Display the peace fruit – the apple – prominently in your home 145

The Chinese like creating the chi of the peace fruit in the home. The word "apple" in Chinese is ping, and this sounds like the word "peace." As a result of this, the apple has always been regarded as having a calming influence when displayed in the home.

Apples have the best effect when they are made from clear glass or crystal, as this simulates the earth energy that is associated with nurturing energy. They are also excellent in this current period of 8, which is an earth period. Hence, for the next 20 years, until February 4 2024, crystals will become increasingly effective in feng shui practice. Collect apples from all over the world – and if you visit New York (the Big Apple) look out for all different types. They have the largest selection of apples there and they also contain the yang energy of that great city. Bring a little bit of that powerful yang energy home with you.

Choose apples of any material – metal, glass, ceramic, wood – as a symbol of peace. Or, have six real red apples on your coffee table for peace and harmony.

146   In a house full of children, place pagodas in strategic corners

If you want your children to be more responsive and less hyperactive, pagodas are excellent symbols to have around the home. They will bring a calming influence to a house full of demanding kids. The pagoda is also symbolic of helping children to bring out the best of their scholarly nature. You will find that they will want to study and to achieve good grades at school; better yet, pagodas – especially when made of a ceramic material or of crystal or glass – are perfect for enhancing their concentration and their sense of focus. Place them in the Northeast corner of their bedrooms. Remember that it is a good idea to have one pagoda per child, or at least one pagoda in each room.

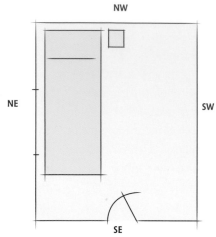

Place a pagoda in the Northeast to help children with homework. Here, the pagoda would be positioned on the window sill to the left of the bed.

147   Enhance schoolwork by tapping good luck directions

Children can sit and sleep in their good directions for personal growth and achievement at school.

Probably the most effective way of bringing out the best of children's studying capabilities is to create a study desk for them that allows them to sit facing their personal growth direction. This is based on their Kua number. Calculate the children's Kua numbers (see Tip 19) and then, using the table here, determine their personal growth directions. Once you have done this, rearrange their bedroom or study room in a way that enables them both to sit facing and to sleep with their heads pointing in the direction indicated. So, the desk and the bed should ideally be placed against the same wall that signifies the best studying direction. Make sure that there are no edges or beams directly above the child's head as he or she works or sleeps.

Good sitting directions for school work

KUA NUMBER	DIRECTION
1	North
2	Southwest
3	East
4	Southeast
5	*
6	Northwest
7	West
8	Northeast
9	South

* Boys with Kua number 5 use Southwest; girls use Northeast.

Watch television sitting on red cushions to ensure goodwill 148

A sure way of avoiding arguments and quarrels between family members in the home, or at least reducing them drastically, is to use red cushions when watching television. You can extend this simple antidote against the manifestation of quarrelling energy by having the color red scattered in any parts of the house where the family tends to congregate – the dining and living rooms, for example, as well as the television room. This is because red suggests fire energy, which exhausts the hostile energy of the quarreling star. This star "flies" all around the house from month to month and you can actually use flying star formulas to calculate where the quarrelling star is located each month.

However, this is troublesome to do as it requires you to be familiar with various feng shui formulas. An easy option, then, is simply to place cures in the house that overcome the quarreling energy and keep them in place throughout the year. This is one of the reasons why the Chinese are so fond of the color red. In addition to it being an auspicious color, red also exhausts all misunderstandings and hostility vibrations in any space.

Have red in communal rooms to keep arguments at bay.

149 Activating peach blossom luck to jumpstart marriage chances

Maximize opportunities for love and marriage by activating helpful astrological animals.

Lonely hearts and forlorn singles . . . anyone who has been repeatedly frustrated in their search for a soul mate or a marriage partner will welcome this easy feng shui way of bringing marriage luck into their life. This method is not for those in search of frivolous fun, however, and it is to be used in addition to the energizing of the Southwest corner of the home with love-enhancing images, such as mandarin ducks, double happiness characters, and the dragon and phoenix symbols. This method is referred to as activating your peach blossom luck.

Animal signs

Start by familiarizing yourself with the astrology wheel, which shows you the compass directions of each of the 12 animal signs (see

Tip 108). This chart is the basis of the Chinese space-enhancement system. You will see that there are 12 animals placed around the compass, and you will also take note that the animal signs make up half of the 24 mountains of the compass, and that every animal symbol is assigned its own compass direction.

The method focuses on the four animal signs that occupy the four cardinal directions of the compass. These are the horse, which occupies the South; the rat, which occupies the North; the rabbit, which occupies the East; and the rooster, which occupies the West. Each of these four animal signs has the power to bring peach blossom marriage luck to a specific group of people born in certain animal signs.

To determine which of these four animals holds the key to unlocking your peach blossom luck, you will need to determine your affinity trinity of animal signs, summarized here.

Peace blossom affinity groups

Group A	Snake, rooster, and ox
Group B	Boar, rabbit, and sheep
Group C	Tiger, dog, and horse
Group D	Monkey, dragon, and rat

Read the Tips that follow for your animal sign.

Creating love opportunities for the snake, rooster, and ox

150

To create peach blossom luck for those people born under the years of the snake, the rooster, and the ox, place an image of the horse in the South of the home and, if you wish, in their bedroom too. It is most important to place the image in the South corner of the home. If this corner corresponds to a toilet or storeroom, however, look for a suitable corner in the garden or in the South of the living room instead. Make sure you get a horse that has jewels and that has been properly made. The more beautiful your horse image is, the better will be the match you are able to manifest.

It is important to be patient. If you are currently dating someone you are fond of but who is fighting shy of making a commitment, you need to understand that the peach blossom luck cannot make him or her want

If you are a rooster, ox, or snake, displaying a horse attracts love luck.

to marry you. It could even trigger a break up in the relationship if there is no destiny affinity between you and your sweetheart. Thus, by breaking off the relationship that is not going anywhere, it could be clearing the way for you to meet your true marriage partner.

Making marriage more possible for the rat, dragon, and monkey

151

Display a rooster to attract love if you are a rat, dragon, or monkey.

For those born in the years of the rat, dragon, or monkey, the animal chi that will unlock your peach blossom luck is the rooster when placed in the West corner of your home or bedroom. The size of the image does not matter, as long as the rooster is beautifully made and is, preferably, adorned with jewels. I have been asked if the gender of the animal sign is relevant, and my answer is "No." After all, you are not activating for a potential spouse who is a rooster, you are actually activating for the peach blossom luck to materialize.

152   Romance luck for the rabbit, sheep, and boar

Those of you born in the years of the rabbit, sheep, or boar should place the image of a rat in the North direction of your home or bedroom in order to activate peach blossom luck. Look for a rat figurine that is well made and, if possible, that resembles the mongoose spewing jewels, or is decorated with crystals that look like jewels.

The quality of decorative features placed in the home to symbolize good feng shui must always be well made and never look like cheap products made of tin and plastic. Bear in mind that symbolism extends to every dimension of the practice.

Shown here is a painting of the Tibetan Buddha of Wealth, the yellow Jambhala, who traditionally is shown holding a rat or a mongoose spouting jewels. If you were born in the year of the rabbit, sheep, or boar, having this painting activates peach blossom luck and wealth luck – so you could end up attracting a wealthy partner! Just make sure to hang it on the North wall of your home.

153   Wedding bells for the horse, dog, and tiger

If you were born in the year of the horse, dog, or tiger, you should place a rabbit image in the East direction if you are seriously looking to settle down and get married. Activating your peach blossom luck will create the situation for you to meet someone with the same intentions, but it does not guarantee the quality of the partner or the longevity of the marriage. These aspects depend on your own destiny and karma.

Feng shui creates the energy chi that is conducive to life being pleasant and happy. It is not magic and cannot be used to change someone's destiny or deepest feelings toward you. Feng shui accounts for only one-third of your luck; the other two-thirds are down to your karmic destiny and the choices you make.

Place a lovable rabbit in the East to jump-start love luck. If possible, get one that is bedecked with jewels – the more valuable it is, the better your catch!

Bonding marriage relationships with amethysts 154

In this period of 8, if you want your love relationship to last, especially if you are already happily married and are not looking for a love triangle, you can strengthen your marriage energy by placing amethyst crystals in the bedroom. Indeed, a powerful Taoist method of bonding husband and wife permanently and making them immune to outside third-party interference is to place a raw amethyst geode under the marriage bed, directly beneath the feet. Then the amethyst is tied with a red string to the bedpost. This has the effect of ensuring that the sleeping couple will not wander into another relationship.

Q & A

Q: *I have a divan bed without legs, so where do I place the amethyst geode?*

A: Unfortunately you cannot use this method, so in this case you might wish to ensure that you are at least sleeping in a direction that ensures that your spouse stays focused on the marriage. The best way to do this is to sleep with your head pointed in your spouse's marriage direction, also known as the nien yen direction (see Tip 19).

Tied to the foot of the bed with red string or ribbon and placed under the woman's side, an amethyst geode helps strengthen relationships by boosting the female energies of earth. This tip also works for men married to a woman who has a roving eye.

155 Why am I still single?

If you are still single and are wondering why, here is a quick list for you to work through to check the feng shui of your home. If you are living alone in your own house or apartment, you should also use the following list to check your parents' home, where you grew up.

- Check your sleeping direction and make sure you are oriented with your head pointed to your nien yen (see Tip 19) or romance direction. If you are sleeping with your head in any other direction you could be hurting your marriage chances, especially if you find that other indications of your romance luck are being blocked.

If you are female and looking for a relationship, check out your art – do not display pictures of lone females, as this just reinforces your current status.

- Check that your astrology location based on your animal sign (see page 11 and Tip 108) is not adversely affected by a toilet or a store room, or is cluttered or afflicted in any other way.

- Check that the Southwest location is not similarly afflicted by the presence of a toilet. This will kill off all romance luck for any eligible people in your home.

- Check that the whole house is not dominated by yin female energy if you are a woman, or by male yang energy if you are a man. When the decoration, art, and other symbols are too yin female or too yang male, they can have a negative effect on your chances of getting married.

Good feng shui to ensure fertility 156

It is also possible to use feng shui to enhance your descendants' luck. This is part of the "happiness" that feng shui is able to bring to families and, indeed, it is regarded as a principal benefit of having good feng shui.

The Laughing Buddha for fertility

An easy way to attract good children luck is to display the image of the Laughing Buddha surrounded by children, or to hang a painting showing one hundred children – this is a famous image in the East. It was always hung in the quarters of the reigning emperors of China, when having many successor princes was of a major concern.

Today, it is possible to find the one-hundred-children image hand-painted onto large crystal balls (you will find them in specialist stores and from wofs.com) which can then be activated by spinning or shining a bright light on them. Adding a large, pink-colored crystal lotus as a decorative feature helps jumpstart baby luck.

Baby images enhance fertility luck and can work wonders for childless couples. Place them in the West, as this the descendants' corner of the home.

Those wanting children activate with 157 a pair of elephants

The traditional symbols that are said to bring children into the household are a pair of elephants shown in the benign posture. In this posture, the elephants should be shown with their trunks down, as depicted here, and they should be placed inside the bedroom near the marital bed. Elephants in the bedroom should, of course, never have their trunks raised as this could inadvertently cause problems for the couple.

They also need not be large – just a pair of small, bedside-sized elephants is sufficient.

158 Feng shui help for childless couples

While fertility symbols are excellent for creating descendants' luck, childless couples who are in need of feng shui help should consider changing their sleeping direction. The correct direction to create family luck for children is for both of you to sleep with your heads pointing in the husband's nien yen direction. This is based on the husband's Kua number (see Tip 19), which you can apply to the table here to determine his nien yen sleeping direction. If you are unable to orientate the bed to produce the correct sleeping direction, try looking for another bedroom in your home where you can. This is what you need to do to help the woman to conceive.

Fertility symbols include fruits, such as pomegranates, but you can further enhance baby luck by positioning your bed in your nien yen, or romance direction – see the chart below.

Kua #	Nien yen direction
1	South
2	Northwest
3	Southeast
4	East
5*	
6	Southwest
7	Northeast
8	West
9	North
* Men with Kua number 5 use Northwest.	

Activating for the golden rice bowl   159

A great working life is one that produces enough money for you and your family to live comfortably, allowing you to meet all your financial obligations. This is often described as having a golden rice bowl. The rice bowl is a metaphor for having enough to eat and to enjoy. In feng shui, the golden rice bowl, which includes the golden chopsticks and golden soup spoon, symbolizes attracting the kind of career luck that brings you a dream job. If you already hold such a position, the symbolism will ensure that you stay long and grow with the job. If you are still striving for that position, then displaying the golden rice bowl, complete with chopsticks and spoon, in the North corner of your home or of your bedroom, will help make it a reality. The North is the career corner and

to find out where the North of your house is, you must use a compass rather than just assume. In Chinese feng shui, orientations must always be determined by a compass.

The golden rice bowl is traditionally presented with a spoon and chopsticks, and symbolizes career luck.

Harmonious sleeping directions for children to   160
prevent squabbling

If you want to ensure that your children do not squabble or indulge in competitive sibling rivalry, make sure that they each sleep with their heads pointing in a direction that is harmonious and beneficial. When children sleep in this auspicious orientation, their chi energy will automatically blend together harmoniously. It is when their sleeping orientations are wrong that trouble could break out. You should not worry about their sleeping orientation for wealth, as they are too young to be activating wealth luck – what they need is the luck of family, as well as the luck of their own personal development and growth.

For children to work and play without fighting, make sure they sleep in their nien yen directions – see the chart in Tip 19.

161   Yang energy-moving lamps for love

In recent years I have seen some pretty stunning new designs for yang energy-moving lamps, or lava lamps. Lava lamps and glitter lamps – these are brightly colored lava lamps with metal strips floating gently inside an oil-filled envelope – are wonderful in feng shui. I knew immediately that they would be perfect for activating the chi energy of any space. They would be especially excellent for keeping the energy of the Southwest moving in an auspicious fashion, thereby creating the energy of nurturing and caring – in other words, love, loyalty, and the nurturing care of matriarchal energy.

Yang benefits

These lamps bring soothing yang chi and I have discovered them to be truly excellent for the bedroom or, in fact, just about anywhere in the home where you want this energy to flourish. You can stare at them for a long time, mesmerized by the moving pieces of metal inside the heated oil. There is a vibrancy about their light and heat they produce that moves the oil, activating the energy of the room, making it alive and happy. I use these lamps as light offerings at my altars and as corner enhancers to keep the energy there moving so it cannot stagnate . . . a very stylish way to practice feng shui – very subtle and very affordable.

Stirring up passion in long-term relationships 162

If you want to stir up the passion in a long-term relationship that seems to have gone sour on you – not because love has flown out the window, but simply because the spark needs re-igniting – you need to employ the symbolism of bright red peony flowers. This is the king of flowers, referred to in Chinese by the name mou tan. Displaying a well-executed painting of the mou tan flower will jumpstart your love life, as it is believed to create the chi vibrations that stirs the loins. The mou tan flower is associated with conjugal love and sexual happiness, so invest in a good-quality peony painting if you want to rekindle those long stagnant desires.

Displaying real peonies or paintings of them enhances love luck.

Ceilings to enhance and transform heaven energy 163

To transform your home into a period of 8 home, thus benefiting from the current period's chi energy, you will also need to change your roof. But if you live in an apartment and find this impossible to do, then you might want to consider installing a new ceiling. This is how you create new heaven energy, and it is definitely one of the requirements for tapping the energy of the current period. In the process of changing the ceiling, you might want to incorporate some circular designs. The circular shape is symbolic of heaven energy and so is especially suitable for the ceiling.

Also, try not to have protruding designs that might appear hostile – always be alert to protrusions sending out harmful energy from above.

Circular ceiling designs harness the energy of heaven. Note that good feng shui always creates the trinity of heaven, earth, and mankind chi, so it is a good idea to ensure yang energy for ceilings.

164   Square floor patterns boost foundation chi

Update your home to period 8 by displaying squares in the floor design, which boosts stability. When you change your flooring it revitalizes the earth energy of your home, which is the most important requirement for transforming your home chi to period 8.

It is a very good idea to create square patterns and designs on ground-level floors, on your driveway outside, or even in your garden as this literally cements in the earth chi of your home. This will ensure that your fortunes stay grounded, giving the stability needed to grow and expand with the years. Earth energy is also excellent in this earth period 8, which will last for nearly another 20 years. So, if you have not done so, change your flooring as part of your plan to transform your home into a period 8 home (see Tip 63) and, in the process, incorporate some square designs into the floors. You can do this even when the floor is carpeted or is made of wood. Be as creative as you wish.

Q & A

Q: *I can't change my carpet, so can I lay down rugs that incorporate squares into the pattern?*

A: Definitely, and this should open your eyes to the designs on carpets. While some of the modern, abstract designs can be attractive, select patterns and designs that also incorporate circles with squares – circles are always good feng shui as they suggest a never-ending source of togetherness and good fortune.

Staircases determine quality of family communication   165

An area of the house that is often forgotten is the staircase. This is a pity because staircase energy is what determines the quality of communication between family members. If you want the interpersonal links between everybody living in the house to be generally harmonious and pleasant, then it is a good idea to ensure that the staircase is showered with good chi. This means keeping the area well lit at all times. It is also a good idea to decorate the walls of the staircase as this will slow down the chi as it makes its way to the next level. In addition, make certain that your staircase does not have any open gaps between the steps. This can cause money to flow out of the house without you realizing it. Keep your staircase solid and happy looking and family members will get on beautifully.

Keep your staircases clean and well lit to promote good communication at home. This is because staircases are places where the energy of the lower (earth) level moves to the upper (heaven) level, so having them auspicious and spacious benefits household residents enormously.

Corridors influence the mood of the home   166

Corridors influence the mood that pervades a home. In fact, it is better not to have corridors in houses and apartments as these tend to be long, narrow walkways with rooms opening off them – which often creates quarrelsome behavior. If you have corridors, then the best type are broad and decorated with colorful art. The idea is to slow down the chi, so paintings and plants are good here as long as they don't cause a blockage of chi. Also, keep corridors well lit, as this creates yang energy which spills into the rooms and adds to the feeling of harmony in the home.

Corridors and halls need to be fresh, airy spaces, or they can bring down the good ambience of your home.

167   Avoid eating from chipped crockery

Eating from chipped crockery is a most inauspicious thing to do, just as drinking from chipped cups or glasses can cause you to experience bad luck. As soon as a plate is chipped, it is best simply to throw it away. This also applies to serving dishes, as serving food from cracked or chipped receptacles is symbolically negative – everything you eat must come from crockery that is intact and untarnished. If you have a dinner service that has sentimental value but which is old and chipped, have it restored or display it as an ornament – but never continue to use it once it is damaged. Examine all the crockery in your home, and immediately discard any that is substandard. This way, you will continue to safeguard the good fortune you have activated through good feng shui practice, rather than negate all your hard work. Attention to detail is the key. Even expensive crystal should be thrown away if the rim of the glass is damaged.

Regularly assess your crockery for cracks and chips, and replace all damaged items to protect your good luck.

168   And finally, protect your dining room

Always pay attention to the dining room. Make sure that you keep this part of your home well ventilated and with no dark, stagnant corners. The dining room symbolizes the place of family wealth-generation, so make sure you do not eat out too often – eating in ensures that good chi is constantly created. Nothing guarantees good feng shui for your house better than serving meals in it regularly. When no food is served for too long, chi stagnates and eventually dies. With activity, laughter, and lots of dining, the chi stays active. This is the crux of good feng shui. Life then becomes pleasant and blissfully calm.

Eating in at home on a regular basis boosts the auspicious luck of the family.

Index

Picture Credits

Page

2 Geoff Dann
3, 4, 5, 6, 7 wofs.com
10 PhotoDisc Inc.
13 Andrew J Smith
14 Andreas von Einsiedel/EWA (Elizabeth Whiting Associates)
15 Tim Street-Porter/EWA
16 Steve Hawkins/EWA
18 Gary Chowenetz/EWA
18 Spike Powell/EWA
20, 21 Getty Images
22 David Giles/EWA (above);
    Edina van der Wyck (below)
23 Rodney Hyett/EWA
24 Spike Powell/EWA. Below: wofs.com
25 Rodney Hyett/EWA.
    Below: Getty Images
26–27 PhotoDisc Inc. art,
28 Rodney Hyett/EWA. Below: wofs.com
29 The Pier
30 Bruce Hemming/EWA
31 Getty Images
32 Getty Images (left); wofs.com (right)
33 Lu Jeffery/EWA (right); below,
    Getty Images
34 Getty Images (left); The Pier (right)
35 PhotoDisc Inc. (left); Getty Images; (right)
36 Ocean
38, 39 40 Getty Images
42 Getty Images (left); wofs.com (right)
43 Tim Street-Porter/EWA
44 Jerry Goldie
45 Tim Street-Porter/EWA
46 Geoff Dann
47 Tim Street-Porter/EWA
52 Getty Images
54 Bruce Hemming/EWA (below);
    wofs.com (above)
57, 58 Getty Images
59 wofs.com (center and right);
    David Giles/EWA (below)
60 Getty Images (above);
    wofs.com (below)
61, 71 Getty Images
62 The Pier (above); Getty Images
    (below); wofs.com (both images
    below right)
63 Getty Images (above);
    wofs.com (below)
64 David Giles/EWA; art, Stephen Dew
65 PhotoDisc Inc.
66 Andrew J Smith; Geoff Dann (detail, top)
67 wofs.com
70 Geoff Dann
72 Brian Hatton
73 Getty Images

75 PhotoDisc Inc; Geoff Dann (detail above)
76 Getty Images; (left); Geoff Dann (below)
77 wofs.com (above); Geoff Dann (below)
78 Getty Images (below)
80 PhotoDisc Inc.; Ocean (below right)
81 Rodney Hyett/EWA
82 David Giles/EWA; wofs.com (right)
83 Geoff Dann
84 wofs.com
85 Tim Street-Porter/EWA
86 Di Lewis/EWA
87, 88, 90, 92 wofs.com
89 Rodney Hyett/EWA
91 Gary Chowenetz/EWA
93, 94, 95, 98 Getty Images
96 Neil Lorimer/EWA
97 Bruce Hemming/EWA
99 Liz Whiting/EWA
100 Adam Papadatos/EWA
101 Dominic Whiting/EWA
102 Di Lewis/EWA
103 Andrew J Smith
104 Liz Whiting/EWA
105 Geoff Dann
106, 108 Getty Images
107 Getty Images; (top); wofs.com (below)
109 Geoff Dan (top)
110 Andrew J Smith
112, 118 Geoff Dann
114, 116, 122 wofs.com
115 Getty Images; wofs.com (below)
117, 119 Getty Images
120 Getty Images; wofs.com (right)
121 Getty Images; wofs.com (left)
124 Getty Images; wofs.com (below)
125 wofs.com; Geoff Dann (right)
126 The Pier; wofs.com (below)
127 Lucinda Symons; wofs.com (below
128 Getty Images; wofs.com (left)
129 Geoff Dann (above);
Heini Schneebeli (below)
131 Tim Street-Porter/EWA
132 Geoff Dann
133 The Pier
134 PhotoDisc Inc.
135 wofs.com; Geoff Dann (below)
136 Mark Luscombe-Whyte/EWA
137, 138 wofs.com
139 Neil Lorimer/EWA; Geoff Dann (left)
140 Jan Baldwin; Ocean (right)
141, 151 wofs.com
142, 143 wofs.com
144 PhotoDisc Inc;
145 Mark Luscombe-Whyte/EWA
146 PhotoDisc Inc.
148 Geoff Dann
149 Bruce Hemming/EWA; wofs.com (right)
150 Tim Street-Porter/EWA; Ocean (below)

152 Ray Main/Mainstream;
    Getty Images (below)
153 wofs.com; PhotoDisc Inc. (below)
154 Geoff Dann
155 Simon Brown
156 Gloria Nicol (left); Geoff Dann (right)
157, 158 Getty Images

Illustrations by Stephen Dew, aside from those by Kate Simunek on pages 13–22, 26, 27, 29, 31, 37, 39, 40, 53, 69, 73, 84, 133, 144; Jacqui Mair, pages 6, 113, 114, 116, 117, 118, 123, 147, 148; Anthony Duke, pages 79, 134; Sarah Perkins, 109, 137, 155; Csaba Pásztor, 92; Ian Midson, 76.

To update your feng shui each year:
Log on to www.wofs.com in February each year to download an annual flying star chart. You will also be able to download monthly updates free of charge. You can also purchase powerful feng shui cures, such as the five-element pagoda, from this website. Note that the art on page 111 (astrology wheel), the flying star charts and eight mansions charts are based on reference supplied by, and the copyright of, Lillian Too.

Lillian Too welcomes all readers to her author website at www.lillian-too.com

Her internet magazine at www.wofs.com

email: ltoo@wofs.com

wofs.com sdn bhd
15th Floor, Menara Millenium
Damansara Heights 50490
Kuala Lumpur
Malaysia
Tel: 603 2080 3466
Fax: 603 2093 3001

The publisher would like to thank:
Mathmos, for the lava lamps shown on page 154.

www.mathmos.com

For photographs:

The Pier
www.pier.co.uk

Ocean
www.oceanuk.com